Equity in the
for Every Child

Equity in the Classroom for Every Child

By

Delia Robinson Richards

Cambridge
Scholars
Publishing

Equity in the Classroom for Every Child

By Delia Robinson Richards

This book first published 2021. The present binding first published 2021.

Cambridge Scholars Publishing

Lady Stephenson Library, Newcastle upon Tyne, NE6 2PA, UK

British Library Cataloguing in Publication Data
A catalogue record for this book is available from the British Library

ISBN (10): 1-5275-6828-8
ISBN (13): 978-1-5275-6828-0

I dedicate *Equity in the Classroom for Every Child* to my brother, Dr. James Fletcher Robinson, a phenomenal scholar, an astounding medical doctor, an inspirational leader and a believer of equitable practices and to our mother, Marian Van Horn Robinson, who always believed in us and encouraged us to strive to achieve our optimal potential.

"That's at the core of equity: **understanding who your kids are and how to meet their needs**. You are still focused on outcomes, but the path to get there may not be the same for each one." (Pedro Noguera)

TABLE OF CONTENTS

ACKNOWLEDGEMENTS

This book's journey was only made possible because of the numerous hours of editing by Compton Richards and Madlynn Anglin, who gave continuous and unparalleled time and energy towards the completion of this book. My University of the District of Columbia Early Childhood student, Camille Beasley, was very conscientious about the completion of the appendix and Gwendolyn Peyton, principal of a District of Columbia Public School, who offered highly instrumental feedback.

I would like to give a heartfelt thanks to my children Patrick, Janelle, Ramon and his wife Erica, along with Alex and Maxwell, who were paramount in being supportive and encouraging on the book' s journey.

Lastly, I would like to thank all my extended family members, colleagues, students, and friends for their belief and confidence in me accomplishing this task. I am grateful for all of you for being in my life.

FOREWORD

My youngest son and I planted seven seeds in a paper cup. He carefully pressed the seeds into the soil, and we added just enough water to sufficiently dampen the soil. Then we placed the cup on a windowsill where the seeds could get good sunlight. About two weeks ago the first stalk began to poke its head through the soil. For the first few days just the one plant was visible. Each day we would excitedly check the plant's progression. Then seemingly overnight, additional stalks began to burst through the soil. Suddenly we were looking at six budding plants, each in various stages of growth, reaching new heights. We marveled at the plants and the workings of nature. Perhaps the most astonishing revelation occurred just the other day when the seventh seed, which we had long since forgotten, began to emerge. As this last tiny bud began its journey, I was reminded that seeds, like children, will bloom in their own time when given the right environment. This knowledge is reassuring as our country is currently navigating tumultuous times.

The global pandemic has forced us to reexamine the ways in which we interact with one another and our environment. What does it mean to have a society grounded in social justice and equity? What role do schools play in keeping our lives and our economy moving forward? Through all of this, teachers find themselves on the front lines. We ask ourselves how can we make the world a safer, more equitable and loving place for our students? How do we protect their futures so that they are given the opportunity to make the world a better place?

Delia Robinson Richards' handbook seeks to equip teachers with the tools they need to face the daunting challenges impacting our country and our classrooms. Her perspective as a seasoned early childhood educator and researcher provides a nuanced voice to the conversation. It is appropriate that we begin by thinking first about Early Childhood Education because this is where our children, our seeds if you will, are first planted and nurtured. We can learn from these practices, regardless of the age group we teach, how to bring our learners into full bloom. This book provides a framework for how teachers might create an equitable teaching and learning environment in which children can thrive.

Just as the seeds my son and I planted needed the essential elements of soil, sun, and water to survive, the seven core values outlined in these chapters are critical for the survival of our children as learners. Chapters 1 and 2, "Time for Change" and "Engaging Students" address the good soil that must be in place for seeds to take root. Teachers must recognize that the status quo is not working for *all* children and we must look for ways to elicit students' active participation and engagement. Chapters 3 and 4, "Appreciating Students' Culture" and "Communicating with Students" serve as the sun that encourages our children to break through the soil and reach new heights of their potential. Teachers are encouraged to recognize and leverage the knowledge students bring into the classroom, while simultaneously presenting them with new concepts and ideas that encourage productive struggle. Chapters 5 and 6, "Helping Students" and "Equalizing Opportunities for Every Child" speak to the necessary, live-giving water that constantly revives the budding plant and helps its root system take hold. Classrooms must be places where students have equal footing, regardless of their life circumstances outside of school. Finally, chapter 8, "Reflecting on Classroom Equity Implementation" focuses on the responsibility of the caretaker who is ever-present and vigilant. Like a skillful gardener, the teacher observes, reflects, and adjusts to maximize the growth and longevity of the budding learners in their care.

The core values discussed in these chapters purposely spell out the acrostic TEACHER. It is the teacher who must till the soil, plant the seeds, and nourish them so that they can grow to their full potential. Dr. Richards has provided a framework that clarifies this work and paves the way for a more equitable learning environment that allows each precious seed to bloom in its own time.

Anika Spratley Burtin, Ph.D.
Associate Professor and Chair,
Division of Education, Health and Social Work
University of the District of Columbia

INTRODUCTION

This handbook demonstrates creating equity in educating each child in the classroom. It is designed to benefit pre-service, novice, and tenured teachers. The purpose of the handbook is to generate support for diverse learners and to give teachers strategies to bridge the achievement gap. It presents a review of literature that supports equity in the classroom for diverse learners. It is focused primarily on the early childhood age group but could easily be adapted to all age groups from K–12th grade.

Teachers can use the handbook as a foundation for ensuring equity in the classroom and across the curriculum. Each chapter of the handbook begins with several questions. The chapter proceeds to answer the questions; however, these questions are a starting point and teachers can add more questions as situations arise or if they feel a need to elaborate on a specific situation.

This handbook consists of the following eight chapters:

Chapter 1 **T**ime for Change
Chapter 2 **E**ngaging Students
Chapter 3 **A**ppreciating Students' Cultures
Chapter 4 **C**ommunicating with Students
Chapter 5 **H**elping Students
Chapter 6 **E**qualizing Opportunities for Students
Chapter 7 **R**eflecting on Equitable Practices in the Classroom
Chapter 8 Summary

The titles of Chapter 1 through Chapter 7 develop an acrostic that spells "TEACHER." Each chapter title indicates a specific core value that should become a part of the teacher's repertoire in the classroom. When these core values are implemented in the classroom, the needs of the diverse learners will be met in addition to empowering teachers and their students. These core values exhibit understanding, appreciation, and respect for diverse learners. The implementation of these core values will create The Blueprint Education Plan (Template 1: The Blueprint Education Plan). This plan will enable the teacher to demonstrate equity for every child in the classroom.

This handbook contributes to the teacher's scholarly and professional development; it can be used as part of the teaching and learning toolbox. Use of it will encourage, support, and impact the attitude and teaching strategies of K–12th grade teachers. It will enable teachers and other educators to support and engage diverse learners in the classroom by using the core values while implementing differentiated strategies that meet the needs of every child.

Today, the term, *Latinos*, is becoming more commonly used to designate a demographically growing group. Several researchers have defined what is meant by the term. Robles de Melendez and Beck[1] use the term Hispanic or Latino to denote an enormous range of people and cultures. Wood[2] refers to *Hispanic* as an umbrella term for anyone of Spanish or Portuguese decent in or outside the U.S. Throughout this book, both terms, Latino and Hispanic, will be used. The U.S. Census Bureau and others use these terms interchangeably although Hispanic refers to native speakers of Spanish or a person who has Spanish-speaking ancestry, whereas Latino refers to anyone of Latin American origin or ancestry.

Boutte[3] suggests that educators should have some level of familiarity with their students' levels of ethnic awareness to better understand them. She describes the five ethnic groups in the US as follows:

- African American—not limited to Black as it also includes African, Caribbean, and Native African.
- Native American/Alaskan Native, which includes over 500 tribes; the largest tribes include Cherokee, Navajo, Sioux, Chippewa/Alout, and Eskimo.
- Asian/Pacific American-largest groups, which include Chinese, Japanese, Korean, Vietnamese, Cambodian, Thai, Filipino, Laotian, Lao-Hmong, Burmese, Samoan, Guamanian, Indonesian, East India, Pakistani, Saudi Arabian, Iranian, Iraqi, and other Arabic-speaking people.
- Latino/American Mexican, Puerto Rican, Cuban, Central and South American.

---

1. Wilma Robles de Melendez and Verna Beck, *Teaching Young Children in Multicultural Classrooms: Issues, Concepts, and Strategies*, 25.
2. Peter Wood, "Hispanics: To Be or Not to Be", 20.
3. Gloria Boutte, Multicultural Education: Raising Consciousness, 21.

- European American English, Welsh, Scottish, German, Dutch, Irish, French, Polish, Russian, Portuguese, Italian, Swiss, Danish, and other European groups.[4]

African America, Latino, Native American and other students have lagged behind their White and Asian peers in math and reading. Howe and Lisi[5] state that, in many instances across the country, there are major discrepancies between the performances of Caucasian students and students of color, as well as between boys and girls. These discrepancies are referred to as the *achievement gap*. According to Irvine,[6] the achievement gap between African American students and their White counterparts is due to a lack of focus on the influences of culture. After over 40 years of attempting to close the achievement gap, Black and Hispanic students still lag behind White and Asian students; the gap persists.[7]

In 2019 according to the National Assessment for Educational Progress (NAEP),[8] a comprehensive measurement of student performance (also known as "The Nation's Report Card"), there was a regression in student proficiency levels in both math and reading in fourth and eighth grades except for a one-point increase in fourth grade math proficiency scores between 2017 and 2019. Students across all ethnic groups posted lower results than their White peers, with low proficiency levels particularly affecting students from low-income families, African American students, and Hispanic students. Nationally, on a scale from 0–500, White students scored 32 points higher (292) on the 2019 eighth grade math assessment than African American students (260). White students also scored 24 points higher than Hispanic students (268) on the same assessment. Among all the students, the average eighth grade math score on the 2019 assessment was 281, well above the average scores for African American and Hispanic students. On the fourth-grade reading assessment for 2019, White students (230) scored 26 points higher than African American students (204), and 21 points higher than Hispanic students (209). The average 2019 fourth grade

---

4. Algae Harrison et al., "Family Ecologies of Ethnic Minority Children", 346-362.
5. William Howe and Penelope Lisi, Becoming a Multicultural Educator: Developing Awareness, Gaining Skills and Taking Action, 7.
6. Jacqueline Jordan Irvine, *Educating Teachers for Diversity: Seeing with a Cultural Eye*, 28-29.
7. Carrie Spector, Stanford Center for Education Policy Analysis. "School poverty— Not Racial Composition—Limits Educational Opportunity, According to New Research From Stanford".
8. National Assessment for Educational Progress (NAEP). "The Results from the 2019 Math and Reading Assessments are Here"!

reading score among all students was 219, a slight drop from 221 in 2017 and higher than the averages posted by African- American and Hispanic students.

This handbook will meet three objectives for teachers in the classroom:

1. Review literature that supports equity in the classroom for diverse learners.
2. Define and apply the seven core values as a construct of the curriculum to support teachers and diverse students.
3. Demonstrate the effectiveness of the seven core values in bridging the achievement gap.

These three objectives will be interwoven with the mission statement.

This book is designed to provide teachers with information to help them create an environment that recognizes that every student is unique, and recognize, appreciate, and respect every student's different cultural background. As the teacher implements the core values from this handbook, the first premise of creating change in the classroom environment will be fulfilled. The school, the student, and the family are interwoven with the core values—the foundation of teaching that will enable each student to reach their optimal potential.

References

Boutte, Gloria. *Multicultural Education: Raising Consciousness.* Belmont: Wadsworth Publishing, 1999.

Harrison, Algae et al. "Family Ecologies of Ethnic Minority Children". *Child Development* 61, no. 2 (1990): 346-362.

Irvine, Jacqueline Jordan, *Educating Teachers for Diversity: Seeing with a Cultural Eye,* New York: Teachers College Press, 2003.

National Assessment for Educational Progress (NAEP). "The Results from the 2019 Math and Reading Assessments Are Here!" U.S. Department of Education, Institute of Education Sciences, 2019. https://nces.ed.gov/nationsreportcard.

Robles de Melendez, Wilma, and Verna Beck. *Teaching Young Children in Multicultural Classrooms: Issues, Concepts, and Strategies.* Albany: Delmar/Thomson Learning, 2007.

Spector, Carrie. Stanford Center for Education Policy Analysis. "School Poverty—Not Racial Composition—Limits Educational Opportunity, According to New Research from Stanford". Stanford: Stanford Center for Education Policy Analysis, September 23, 2019. https://news.stanford.edu/2019/09/23/new-data-tool-shows-school-poverty-leads-racial-achievement-gap/.

Wood, Peter. "Hispanics: To Be or Not to Be". In *Race and Ethnic Relations: Annual Editions 94/95* edited by John A. Kromkowski. Guilford: Dushkin, 1994.

CHAPTER 1

TIME FOR CHANGE

The first core value represented in the TEACHER acrostic is *Time for Change*. The student achievement gap has been the same for nearly 50 years.[1] However, the American education system has attempted to bridge this education achievement gap for over four decades. Some questions come to mind as we continue to strive to end this achievement gap. These questions are necessary to move forward with this endeavor. These questions are related to research on the achievement gap and the critical role of the teacher in the classroom:

- What are the results from some of the research on bridging the achievement gap?
- How is the research addressing teachers in terms of bridging the achievement gap?
- How will teacher biases be addressed?
- How will teachers implement time changes?
- What changes will close the achievement gap?

Results of Research on the Achievement Gap

On April 14, 2008, Debra Viadero[2] researched the Black-White achievement gap in the United States and discovered the brightest African American children were losing academic ground. This loss indicated that, as students move from elementary and middle schools, the test-gap widens. Researchers who have studied the achievement gap were not surprised with this data outcome because, for a long time, research has shown this disparity.[3] In

---

1. The Harvard Gazette, "Student Achievement Gap Same After Nearly 50 Years, Study Says".
2. Debra Viadero, "Black-White Gap Widens Faster for High Achievers".
3. National Assessment for Educational Progress (NAEP), "School Composition and the Black–White Achievement Gap".

addition to the achievement gap results, African American students are underrepresented among the top scorers on standardized tests.[4]

Sean F. Reardon from Stanford University analyzed the reading and math test scores of 7,000 elementary students from kindergarten to 5th grade.[5] This research indicated the achievement gap grew twice as fast among the students who started out performing above the mean than among lower-performing children. Mr. Reardon concluded that if these gaps continue to grow throughout a child's schooling, even if the child demonstrates high levels of readiness in kindergarten, they will still end up falling below the high performing students.

In contrast, John B. Diamond, a Harvard Associate Professor who is not connected to the two studies, stated that "educational opportunities intertwine to reinforce the racial achievement gap".[6] He explained that educational opportunities need to be identified to see the differences.

Howard[7] noted that the U.S. demographic population is rapidly changing, and a variety of achievement indicators show that the teaching practices and procedures that seemed to work in the past with a predominately White student population are no longer appropriate for a more diverse student population. He continued to explain that indicators such as standardized test scores and graduation rates are lower among students who are poor, while dropout rates are higher. These students have lower grades and more failing grades on average than White students. Poor minority students tend to graduate in lower numbers and drop out of school in higher numbers. The gap or disparity in achievement has been a cause for alarm.[8]

According to the Harvard Civil Rights Project, Frankenberg, Lee, and Orfield[9] stated the widening achievement gap between White students and African-American and Latino students showed that the statistics about

---

4. National Assessment for Educational Progress (NAEP), "Achievement Gaps".
5. Sean Reardon, "The Widening Academic Achievement Gap Between the Rich and the Poor: New Evidence and Possible Explanations".
6. John Diamond, "Still Separate and Unequal: Examining Race, Opportunity and School Achievement in Integrated Schools".
7. Tyrone Howard, *Why Race and Culture Matters in Schools: Closing the Achievement Gap in America's Classrooms*, 134.
8. Linda Darling-Hammond and John Bransford (eds.), *Preparing Teachers for a Changing World: What Teachers Should Learn and Be Able to Do*.
9. Erica Frankenberg, Chungmei Lee, and Gary Orfield, *A Multiracial Society with Segregated Schools: Are We Losing the Dream?*, 11-12.

achievement test results, dropout rates, and the growing school violence indicate that a different approach to the process of teaching and learning must be instituted to benefit all students. Pertinent insights into the impact of the achievement gap from the Harvard Civil Rights Project include the following:

- Minority children are overrepresented in special education.
- African American and Native American students in affluent White districts are labelled as mentally retarded more than their White counterparts.
- There is a higher incidence of suspensions among African American students than among their White counterparts.
- Dropout rates are distinctly higher among urban students of color.
- High school graduation rates are distinctly lower among urban students of color.

Some of the key findings were that extremely disadvantaged students are three to four years behind their more affluent peers. Frankenberg, Lee, and Orfield[10] continue stating that standardized test scores were lower among African American, Latino, and Native American than their White counterparts. Going to college and graduating were also lower. In addition, poverty, drug and alcohol abuse, teen pregnancies, incarceration, hate crimes, bias, prejudice, and discrimination were high among African Americans, Latinos, and Native American students. This list is alarming: the project was compiled in 2003 and the state of education has not improved 16 years later as education in the United States is still facing the same concerns.

An article dated March 19, 2019, titled "Student Achievement Gap Same After Nearly 50 Years", reviewing national and world affairs, stated that the achievement gap for math, reading, and science tests between disadvantaged and well-off students is as wide as it was in 1954.[11] Paul E. Peterson, Professor of Government at Harvard and a member of the research team, collected data on four national assessments, which included 98 tests administered over 47 years to more than 2.7 million students between 14 and 17 years old. Some of the key findings[12] indicated:

---

10. Erica Frankenberg, Chungmei Lee, and Gary Orfield, *A Multiracial Society with Segregated Schools*, 11-12.
11. The Harvard Gazette, "Student Achievement Gap Same After Nearly 50 Years, Study Says".
12. The Harvard Gazette, "Student Achievement Gap Same After Nearly 50 Years".

- extremely disadvantaged students were three to four years behind their more affluent peers;
- the opportunity gap has not wavered over the last half-century; and
- the gaps between other student subgroups also remain nearly constant (i.e., race remains a factor, as the Black-White achievement gap has plateaued for the past quarter-century).

Overall performance improves among 14-year-old students over time, but these gains fade by age 17. However, there have been some success stories in schools attempting to close the achievement gap.

Success Stories that Narrowed or Closed the Achievement Gap

The U.S. Department of Education[13] reported some lessons from successful schools regarding closing the achievement gap. The four study schools across the US included:

- Del Valle High School in El Paso, Texas, which had a 97% Hispanic population. Staff closed the achievement gap in mathematics by ensuring that the Hispanic students at the school passed the Texas Assessment of Academic Skills in 2002 at the same rate as White students.
- El Camino High School in Oceanside, California, which had a population of 3,000 students. Staff were able to narrow the achievement gap for Hispanic students in mathematics and reading with a 24-percentage point reduction in the mathematics achievement gap and a 14-percentage point decrease in reading.
- Florin High School in Sacramento, California, which narrowed the achievement gap in reading by 10 percentage points for African American students and 14 percentage points for Hispanic students.
- North Central High School in Indianapolis, Indiana, which narrowed its achievement gap in English, languages, and the arts by 10 percentage points and in mathematics by 15 percentage points for African American students.

---

13. Shelley Billig et al., "Closing the Achievement Gap: Lessons from Successful Schools".

The U.S. Department of Education[14] held a focus group with administrators and teachers to discuss how they managed to close or narrow the achievement gap. The common themes related to school culture, curriculum and instruction, and leadership for change were identified. They included the following:

School Culture

- High expectations for student achievement: that included eliminating remedial classes and recommending minority students enroll in advance and honor courses.
- Learning supports put in place to help students meet expectations that included tutoring, study skills programs, and ongoing personalized attention from teachers.
- Teachers receiving professional development training for effective reading and math teaching strategies.
- Emphasis on accountability and assessment to determine when students need additional help.
- Analyzing assessments to guide changes in curriculum and instruction.
- Seeing what teaching strategies work best with specific populations of students.
- A collaborative and optimistic attitude that included collaborative efforts from teachers, parents, and community members, not accepting excuses, and being passionate and enthusiastic about improving the students' accomplishments.

Curriculum and Instruction

- Curriculum alignment and standards-based instruction. All participants stressed the importance of teaching to the state and district content standards that reflect knowledge and skills in the content areas.
- State and district assessments were aligned to the school curriculum and the state and local standards.
- Changes in class schedules that allowed more time for instruction. Longer blocks of time for some courses, such as Algebra I, to allow time for instruction and for students to practice skills.

---

[14] Shelley Billig et al, "Closing the Achievement Gap: Lessons from Successful Schools, 42.

- Engaging teaching techniques. Teachers realized students learn better when instruction is individualized, incorporates hands-on teaching techniques, and utilizes strategies that specifically teach students how to take notes, organize their thinking, and solve problems. Technology was also used to engage students.

Leadership for Change

- Change is difficult, but necessary. Educators recognized change was necessary to improve Hispanic and African American students' achievement levels. These educators were motivated to ensure that all students succeed.
- Leadership and resources. Sometimes teachers led and, at other times, the administrators performed the task, but both groups knew what was needed: sufficient resources, time for professional development, material acquisitions, and student support services.
- Federal and state policies serve as catalysts. National, state, and local levels served as a motivator for change, but the specific changes were based on local decisions.

These were some of the leadership changes that occurred in the high schools. The changes varied but had similarities in the four high schools. Changes occurred locally through educators and administrators. A strategic plan now guides all activities and is monitored by the community, staff, and students. In one of the schools, teams were formulated along with a written plan that inspired greater commitment and facilitated change from the other staff members. The teachers were placed in teams and developed a portfolio with learning objectives and goals for their specific grade. The teachers discussed the portfolios on a regular basis.

The district provided support in various ways in the four schools. In one of the schools, the district provided funding for substitute teachers to support the time needed for vertical planning for the teaching teams. In another school, the district facilitated change by helping with monitoring but otherwise served as a resource for removing impediments rather than as a leader for change.[15]

---

15. Shelley Billig et al, "Closing the Achievement Gap: Lessons from Successful Schools".

Overview of the Collaborative Effort in the Four Schools

The teachers in the focus group[16] spoke of the many meetings and dialogues that occurred over lunch and created space to discuss how to improve achievement overall as well as for specific students. Parents and community members were also involved in sharing their culture of success through frequently donating time and funds, working with students at home, and providing the time and effort required to get students to Saturday and summer programs. The teachers were enthusiastic, although many times there was a small group of motivated teachers who collaborated to create change and then, eventually everyone came onboard.

Principals set the tone for high expectations for staff as well as students. Administrators provided support, such as professional development and schedule changes to give longer blocks of time to facilitate instruction in critical content areas. The teachers and administrators discussed the importance of aligning the curriculum with the state and district standards and tests. Two of the schools' staff used the alignment process along with an examination of test scores and classroom observations to decide the most important standards to address. In addition, staff from all the schools examined the performance of a subpopulation of students to determine which reading and math topics needed to be reviewed and taught differently.[17]

Addressing teachers' research indicated that the teacher is the most important component in bridging the achievement gap. Saphier[18] explained that, of all the things that are important to having good schools, nothing is as important as teachers and what they know, believe, and do. Also, Irvine[19] noted how the lack of achievement among African- American students can be attributed to the quality of their teacher.

---

16. Shelley Billig et al, "Closing the Achievement Gap: Lessons from Successful Schools".
17. Shelley Billig et al, "Closing the Achievement Gap: Lessons from Successful Schools".
18. Jon Saphier, *Bonfires and Magic Bullets: Making Teaching a True Profession*, 49-50.
19. Jacqueline Jordan Irvine, *Educating Teachers for Diversity: Seeing with a Cultural Eye*, 71.

In addition, Corbett and Wilson [20] recorded the results from interviews of nearly 400 students from low-income urban schools. The students agreed that the quality of their school experiences depended on good teaching. The students characterized "superior" instructors as those who instituted an overall high-quality professional mission and instructional techniques that included:

- enforced expectations that students complete their work,
- effectively managed the classroom,
- available to assist any student that needed help,
- offered to clearly explain content and subsequent assignments,
- provided varied classroom activities, and
- demonstrated caring by getting to know their students.

The conclusion was these techniques greatly benefit students and ensure success in urban classrooms. Melser[21] reported that some preservice teachers spent a semester experiencing student teaching in an Indianapolis public school with an enrollment of 89% African American. The teachers learned how difficult it was to teach students they had not yet connected with. The preservice teachers created an event called Family Fun Night, where families, parents, and community members came into the school to learn about what the students were being taught. This provided rich professional growth and facilitated relationships among the teachers, families, students, and the community. After this event, the preservice teachers felt they knew how to celebrate and assist students in learning to the best of their ability; they knew they could make a positive difference when teaching diverse students.

This preservice teacher experience coincides with Delpit and Roman's research. Delpit[22] explained that culturally diverse students find themselves at a disadvantage for many reasons, including the fact that teachers do not attempt to find out who the students really are. In addition, teachers are not encouraged to develop links to the often-rich home lives of their other students. Teachers cannot hope to begin to understand who sits before them if they have not connected with their students' families and communities.

---

20. Dick Corbett and Bruce Wilson, "What Urban Students Say About Good Teaching". 18-22.
21. Nancy Melser, "Ain't Nothin' Like the Real Thing: Preparing Teachers in an Urban Environment", 228.
22. Lisa Delpit, *Other People's Children: Cultural Conflict in the Classroom*, 182.

As Roman[23] indicated, having knowledge about another culture does not mean to only speak one or two words in a student's language or to celebrate an activity or sing a song based on the student's heritage. Being sensitive to another's culture requires making changes in one's curriculum or pedagogy when the students' needs have not been served. It requires being patient, tolerant, curious, creative, and eager to learn and, most importantly, non-authoritarian with students. For a teacher to promote excellence in education, there must be a real and honest connection between the teacher and the students' cultural values.

Teacher Bias

For change to occur, teachers need to be transparent with themselves, know themselves, and be honest about any biases that they may possess. Once teachers can discuss their biases, they become able to move forward and acquire the core values that are needed to build equity in the classroom and to close the achievement gap.

Kopetz, Lease, and Warren-King[24] explained that teachers need to understand the socioeconomic conditions that are most prevalent in urban schools in order to adjust and design teaching and learning to effectively meet the needs of a diverse student population. It becomes evident that elevating the achievements of students of color will not happen until teachers are trained to place students and culture at the center of learning.[25]

In addition, teachers must first understand their own cultures before they can appreciate and use their students' cultures in effective instruction.[26] According to Villegas and Lucas,[27] teaching students from culturally and linguistically diverse backgrounds, especially marginalized groups, requires

23. Leslie Roman, "Social Class, Language, and Learning", 90-97.
24. Patricia Kopetz, Anthony Lease, and Bonnie Warren-Kring, *Comprehensive Urban Education*, 195.
25. William Howe and Penelope Lisi, *Becoming a Multicultural Educator: Developing Awareness, Gaining Skills and Taking Action*, 7, 49-50.
26. Kikanz Nuri-Robins et al., *Culturally Proficient Instruction: A Guide for People Who Teach*, cited by Howe & Lisi, *Becoming a Multicultural Educator, 111.*
27. Ana Maria Villegas and Tamara Lucas, "Culturally Responsive Teachers", 204-207.

a new way of teaching. Villegas and Lucas[28] developed a coherent framework with six salient qualities:

- understanding how learners construct knowledge,
- learning about students' lives,
- being conscious of sociocultural issues,
- holding affirming views about diversity,
- teaching ethical activities, as teachers have an ethical obligation to help all children learn, and
- using appropriate instructional strategies.

Approaching students' education in culturally and responsive ways rather than emphasizing deficits has the potential to engage all students in learning. The teacher must be intentional about building equity in the classroom by being inclusive in a positive manner and building on each students' strengths. It also means appreciating and respecting the diverse cultures in the classroom and ensuring that each child has the necessary support to reach their maximum potential.

Time Changes for Teachers

For teachers to implement the Blueprint Education Plan, the time that has already been developed and implemented into the classroom schedule will have to be adjusted (Template 1). The core values involve more individualized instructions and support for students to meet their optimal potential. More time will be needed since there are diverse learning styles in the classroom, and the teacher will need to equalize the learning field to abolish the inequities that have existed in the classroom.

These accommodations may include getting more helping hands in the classroom. Flexibility needs to be built into the schedule as some content areas may last longer than others and, where the concepts are easier for students to grasp, less time may be needed. Students may work individually with support from the teacher or classroom helper on some concepts that may be more challenging. Since being intentional about building equity for all students is a change, teachers must have some mandatory intentional professional development. Professional development may include topics such as: building self-concept in students; the importance of multicultural education; understanding students' diverse backgrounds; and incorporating

---

28. Ana Maria Villegas and Tamara Lucas, "Culturally Responsive Teachers," 205-206.

multiple intelligences theory into the curriculum. Some of the concepts in the lessons from the selected schools illustrate an overlap with the core values. The idea of administrators and teaching staff working together and being enthusiastic may be the starting point for ensuring school success in meeting the needs of all students. This Blueprint Education Plan (Template 1) requires time for discussion, exchanging ideas, asking questions, giving support, and involving parents. All staff members must be ready for change to close the achievement gap and help each student reach their maximum potential.

Chapter Summary

Although the American education system has attempted to bridge the education gap, there has been a student achievement gap for over 40 years. Researchers have demonstrated that this achievement gap was not a surprise because, for a long time, research has revealed the disparity that African-American, Latino and other students of color were and are still underrepresented among the top scorers in standardized tests, such as those reported by the NAEP.

The research that has been cited in this chapter can be used for the blueprint to close the achievement gap. The disparities (dropout rates, low standardized test scores, and low graduation rates) cited by the researchers would be eliminated if the seven core values are implemented along with the techniques explained by the U.S. Department of Education's four study high schools. We will also be delving into other research in the following chapters. This will create the Blueprint Education Plan (Template 1) that will resolve the major disparity in American schools: The Bridging of the Achievement Gap. This Blueprint Education Plan is applicable to K–12th grade. Teachers can tweak the plan to ensure that it is age-appropriate for their specific group of students.

References

Billig, Shelley et al. "Closing the Achievement Gap: Lessons from Successful Schools". Washington: U.S. Department of Education, Office of Vocational and Adult Education, 2005. https://Closing the Achievement Gap Focus Group meeting (MS WORD) (ed.gov).

Corbett, Dick, and Bruce Wilson. "What Urban Students Say About Good Teaching". *Educational Leadership* 60, no. 1 (2002): 18-22.

Darling-Hammond, Linda, and John Bransford (eds.). *Preparing Teachers for a Changing World: What Teachers Should Learn and Be Able to Do.* San Francisco: Jossey-Bass, 2005.

Delpit, Lisa. *Other People's Children: Cultural Conflict in the Classroom.* New York: New Press, 1996.

Diamond, John, "Still Separate and Unequal: Examining Race, Opportunity and School Achievement in Integrated Schools". *The Journal of Negro Education* 75, no. 3 (2006): 495. http://www.jstor.org/stable/40026817.

Frankenberg, Erica, Chungmei Lee, and Gary Orfield. *A Multiracial Society with Segregated Schools: Are We Losing the Dream?* (Cambridge: Civil Rights Project, Harvard University, 2003).

Howard, Tyrone. *Why Race and Culture Matters in Schools: Closing the Achievement Gap in America's Classrooms.* New York: Teachers College Press, 2010.

Howe, William, and Penelope Lisi. *Becoming a Multicultural Educator: Developing Awareness, Gaining Skills and Taking Action.* Oakland: Sage, 2020.

Irvine, Jacqueline Jordan, et al. (2006). *Comprehensive Urban Education.* Boston: Pearson Education, 2006.

Melser, Nancy. "Ain't Nothin' Like the Real Thing: Preparing Teachers in an Urban Environment," *Childhood Education* 82, no. 5 (2006): 228-231.

National Assessment for Educational Progress (NAEP). School Composition and the Black–White Achievement Gap. July 2015. https://nces.ed.gov/nationsreportcard/subject/studies/pdf/school_comp osition_and_the_bw_achievement_gap_2015.pdf

Nuri-Robins, Kikanz et al. *Culturally Proficient Instruction: A Guide for People Who Teach*, 3rd ed. Thousand Oaks: Corwin, 2012.

Reardon, Sean F. "The Widening Academic Achievement Gap Between the Rich and the Poor: New Evidence and Possible Explanations". In *Whither Opportunity? Rising Inequality, Schools, and Children's Life Chances*, edited by Greg Duncan and Richard Murnane Russell, 91-116. Thousand Oaks: Sage, 2011. http://www.jstor.org/stable/10.7758/9781610447515

Roman, Leslie. "Social Class, Language, and Learning," in *The Light in Their Eyes: Creating Multicultural Learning Communities,* edited by Sonia Sonia Nieto (New York: Teachers College Press, 1999), 90-97.

Saphier, Jon. *Bonfires and Magic Bullets: Making Teaching a True Profession.* Carlisle: Research for Better Teaching, 1994.

The Harvard Gazette. "Student Achievement Gap Same After Nearly 50
    Years, Study Says". March 18, 2019.
    https://news.harvard.edu/gazette/story/2019/03/harvard-researcher-
    colleagues-student-achievement-gap-unchanged-in-nearly-50-years.
Viadero, Debra. "Black-White Gap Widens Faster for High Achievers",
    Education Week, April 14, 2008. https://www.edweek.org/policy-politics
    /black-white-gap-widens-faster-for-high-achievers/2008/04?tmp=
    11285675
Villegas, Ana Maria, and Tamara Lucas, "Culturally Responsive Teachers."

CHAPTER 2

ENGAGING STUDENTS

The second core value represented in the TEACHER acrostic is *Engaging Students*. Teachers should be intentional when engaging the children in the classroom. This means making sure that every child is engaged in all the activities, such as presentations, asking and answering questions, and sharing homework assignments. The following questions should be answered when considering how to engage students in the classroom:

- Who are your students and families?
- What are your students' skill levels?
- What type of learner is each one of your students?
- What resources are needed for each of your students to reach their optimal potential?
- What will motivate each student to want to participate in the activities?

Knowing Your Students and Their Families

Every school year is different for a teacher. No school year is the same, even if a teacher is teaching the same age group or grade level. Teachers should send a questionnaire or a survey home, such as the "All About Me" profile for each child, which asks questions about the student (Templates 2 and 3). If the students are older, the teacher can let them complete this survey in class.

As the teacher reviews the "All About Me" profiles from the parents/caregiver and from the student, they can begin to integrate the things each student likes into their curriculum (Templates 2 and 3: All About Me). If possible, the teacher needs to review the profile with the parent to ensure full understanding of the responses. The profile should be broad enough to encompass the students' beliefs and values related to their diverse cultures. The students will gravitate towards familiar concepts and feel like they are a part of the curriculum. In other words, although the curriculum is already developed, its implementation can be personalized to meet the needs of the children in the classroom.

An example of this form of implementation is picture books that you can order or make with the child's name in the story (Template 4: Child's Picture Book). The student becomes the main character of the picture book. Sometimes, the book may also contain the name of the student's dog or other things in the student's environment, which really personalizes the story. Other examples of personalizing teaching are if the teacher knows a student loves music or has an aquarium, then these can be incorporated into lessons. An additional example is buying photo album books from the Dollar Store so that the students can make their own books with pictures that have been brought from home or taken at school. The students can label each picture with a sentence to describe the photograph.

When the teacher sends the "All About Me" profile home, they can also include a profile describing the teacher (Template 5: Meet the Teacher). This could be in the form of a biographical sketch about the teacher. This assignment will then have become a two-way communication venue. It is a way for a student and their family to build a rapport with the teacher since the teacher is doing the same with the student. Also, it is a way to build engagement among the teacher, the child, and the family. In this way, the school year begins with a strong communication foundation. It is exceedingly difficult to teach and meet the students' academic needs if you do not know who you are teaching.

In a single family, with the same biological mother and father, each child will, nevertheless, be different. If these differences exist in one family, there are even more differences in a classroom with many different families and, as we know, every child is unique. As the teacher begins to know the children and families in the classroom, appreciating and respecting their differences, values, and beliefs is critical.

Klein and Chen[1] reported that "the importance of family involvement in children's schooling cannot be overstated. Early childhood professionals must provide information and strategies to non-mainstream parents regarding ways of interacting with their children that will help close the literacy gap before they enter kindergarten." The first 5 years provide the foundation of an education.

---

1. Diane Klein and Deborah Chen, *Working with Children Culturally Diverse Backgrounds*, 190.

Of course, families value teachers and want to work with them to help their child reach their maximum potential. The whole multicultural concept is a part of the "All About Me" task. It is interesting to note that sometimes there can be many similarities among people, even though they may be from a different cultural background. When parents and families know that the teacher has an interest in who they are, it will make a major difference in the bond that can be developed between the teacher, the student, and their family.

Grant and Ray[2] maintained high quality family engagement programs improve and support student achievement. When families are involved in the student's education, then students will demonstrate the following:

- Earn higher grades and test scores,
- Be less likely to be retained in a grade,
- Be more likely to have an accurate diagnosis for an educational placement,
- Attend school regularly,
- Like school and adapt well to it,
- Have better social skills,
- Have fewer negative behavior reports, and
- Graduate and enter post-secondary education.

A classroom environment that has been built on family expectations will help the teacher motivate and instill positive self-esteem in their students. The classroom has now become an extension of the home. The whole idea of engaged families will easily transition to the child being engaged in the classroom. This becomes a natural phenomenal in the classroom. The teacher must also understand, appreciate, and respect every student's uniqueness and their cultural differences. Since this is the framework of the classroom, students will be involved and become its cornerstone. As the teacher builds on the student's uniqueness, it translates into an understanding that will benefit the student and, subsequently, develop them into the best that they can be, not only academically but as a whole person.

Now that the teacher has developed and implemented concepts from the "All About Me" profile, the classroom's foundation has been set. This foundation involves engaging all students by developing a positive rapport with the students and their families. It demonstrates that every child is important and that their cultural background underpins what and how they

---

2. Kathy Grant and Julie Ray, *Home, School, and Community Collaboration*, 8.

learn in the classroom. This foundation demonstrates the teacher's appreciation and respect for all students and their families.

The Students' Skill Levels

In many schools, at the beginning of the school year students will be tested to find out their skill level, particularly in math and reading. As the students are tested, the teacher should note that using just one test to determine the students' performance may not be accurate. Written tests are the most commonly used form of assessment to determine how a student performs academically. Additional diverse assessments could confirm the student's performance level more accurately. These assessments may include informal as well as non-traditional assessments that are related to the student's learning style.

Saunders, Velasco, and Oakes[3] suggested that the achievement gap, which was based on standardized test scores for high- and low-income students, demonstrated that there has been an increase in the number of students enrolling in college from more affluent families, while the number of students entering college from less affluent families has remained static. Affluent parents can provide resources, networks, and opportunities for their children to ensure that they are college-bound, but less affluent parents do not have access to these opportunities.

One consideration that teachers should be aware of is that some students do not test well. The test is no doubt accurate, but it is important that we consider all the test factors that can affect how a student performs, such as their health, nutrition, test anxiety, and environmental issues. Health issues may refer to a student having a fever, cold, stomachache, or allergy. Often, students are sent to school when they are not feeling well. In addition, what if the student has not had breakfast that morning? Being hungry and trying to concentrate on taking a test is a difficult task not to mention all the effects of having cold or allergy symptoms. These are conditions that are real but are often not considered. Test anxiety can also be a problem for some students who lack confidence and have never been taught test-taking strategies. Environmental issues are situations that plague some students' homes or neighborhoods, such as drugs, poverty, and crime. These, too, can have a negative impact on a student's test performance.

---

3. Marisa Saunders, Jorge Ruiz De Valasco, and Jeannie Oakes, "Introduction", 3-5.

Saunders, Valance, and Oakes[4] discuss factors in children's lives that contribute to growing up with access to few resources. These factors include access to a high-quality preschool, enrichment activities, medical care, housing stability, and trauma. In areas where poverty is highly concentrated, there will also be limited resources.[5] This is where inequities in education become visible. The students' living environments are not equal. It is beneficial for the students if their teacher takes these factors into consideration and attempts to remedy them.

Keeping healthy snacks and water in the classroom will help to deal with students' hunger and thirst. Teachers should take a few minutes to perform a health check on each student every morning when they first enter the classroom (Template 6: Daily Quick Health Check). A daily health check is a quick way to indicate a change in a child's health or well-being. This quick health check includes all of the child's physical aspects, such as looking for changes in mood, feeling for a fever, listening to the child's complaints, or detecting an unusual smell. A health form is provided in English and Spanish by the National Resource Center for Health and Safety in Childcare.[6]

Having clothing and food banks somewhere in the school could help parents who have difficulty buying food and clothing. This assistance will indirectly help students so that they can reach their optimal potential. These banks would have to be inconspicuous to avoid any stigma attached to using these supports. Often when students are not performing well academically, the system will categorize them as not achieving based on a grade level; however, these environmental factors must be considered and alleviated in order for the students to be judged accurately. Factors, such as poor health, inadequate nutrition, and home/neighborhood trauma, will affect a student's academic performance in school. These factors are not the student's fault; however, they do affect their educational outcomes.

Hale,[7] has concluded that inferior educational outcomes are tolerated for African American children every day in inner city, suburban, and private school settings. The data on student achievement supports Hale's conclusions. African American, Latino, and American Indian students are not meeting

---

4. Marisa Saunders, Jorge Ruiz De Valasco, and Jeannie Oakes, "Introduction", 3-5.
5. Cameron Brenchley, "Equity and Excellence Commission Delivers Report to Secretary Duncan".
6. National Resource Center for Health and Safety in Childcare.
7. Janice Hale, *Learning While Black: Creating Educational Excellence for African American*, cited by Donna Gollnick and Philip Chinn, *Multicultural Education in a Pluralistic Society* 74.

standards according to the standardized tests required in most states. As a result, a disproportionately large number of students of color are not being promoted to the next grade, not graduating from high school, and dropping out of school.[8] As teachers place students according to their test scores, they should keep in mind the inequities that may prevail. Teacher should also be aware that the placement could be skewed because of the factors that have been discussed. As a result, there are additional kinds of assessments that should be administered to identify the most appropriate placement.

Student Learning Styles

Teachers should know that every child is different. Teachers need to consider all of the differences within their classroom, as what is being taught should reflect how their students learn. Once again, it is important to be intentional about how and what is being taught because students can be visual, auditory, or kinesthetic learners. The integration of Howard Gardner's Theory of Multiple Intelligences[9] can be extremely instrumental in enabling all students to achieve. The website, verywellmind.com, [10] defines each of the nine intelligences, such as visual-spatial, linguistic-verbal, intrapersonal, and interpersonal. Gardner proposed that individuals may possess one or more of the nine forms of intelligence.

Richards[11] collected and analyzed data from a study that explored the integration of the Multiple Intelligences Theory in an elementary school near Atlanta, Georgia. The conclusion was that, when the Multiple Intelligences Theory is integrated into the curriculum, it results in differentiated instruction that enhances and builds on children's strengths and love for learning. It categorizes students into different kinds of learners according to the type of intelligence that best describes them. When teachers intentionally implement the Multiple Intelligences Theory into the curriculum, every student is rewarded. Students will learn concepts using their learning style. Applying this theory demonstrates every child's uniqueness in the classroom. The Multiple Intelligences Theory also reminds students that everyone is different and learning concepts can vary with each student. Indirectly, the theory reflects the students' importance, and that, although

---

8. Donna Gollnick and Philip Chinn, *Multicultural Education in a Pluralistic Society*, 74-77.
9. Kendra Cherry, "Howard Gardner's Theory of Multiple Intelligences".
10. Kendra Cherry, "Howard Gardner's Theory of Multiple Intelligences".
11. Delia Richards, "The Integration of the Multiple Intelligence Theory into the Early Childhood Curriculum", 1096-1099.

each student is different, it is critical for them to learn the lessons that are being taught. This way of teaching is individualized, but it is also collective. The implementation of the theory is demonstrating using students' learning style and differentiating teaching methods while demonstrating that each student is being introduced to the same concepts. The idea of multiple intelligence is to show students that they are important, that their learning style has been identified, and that they will learn the concepts that are being taught. The integration of the Multiple Intelligence Theory sets a positive foundation for everyone. It shows students that they will reach their maximum potential and that the curriculum incorporates how they learn and retain concepts. This integration of the theory is a different teaching approach that will help all students benefit from what is being taught.

Irvine[12] concluded in her work that there are many teachers who make a difference in reversing the cycle of despair and school failure among African American and other non-mainstream students. The current ideal is to provide support to teachers who are having difficulty in making a positive connection with children of color. The implementation of Multiple Intelligences Theory has leveled the playing field as it eliminates the inequities that exist in education. This system avoids the incorrect notion that the color of your skin, who you are, or where you live dictates your grade level and ability to achieve. Gollick and Chin[13] called this notion a self-fulfilling prophecy, which is when the teacher develops instruction and interactions with their students that results in the students behaving as the teacher's expected. As a result, quickly dividing the class into groups by the third week of school suggests the teacher has limited knowledge about the students' academic abilities as this decision is, at least partially, based on biased expectations.

Although we do not verbalize these kinds of feelings to our students, they will easily feel that they are different, inferior, and inadequate. A child will feel very defeated if they are not being treated fairly compared to the other students in the classroom. However, if a student goes into a classroom and knows that the teacher's help, support, kindness, and caring attitude is in their favor, they cannot help but do well. It has been over 50 years since Brown vs. the Board of Education[14] said that the segregation of public

---

12. Jacqueline Jordan Irvine, *Educating Teachers for Diversity: Seeing with a Cultural Eye*, 3-9, 27.
13. Donna Gollick and Philip Chinn, *Multicultural Education in a Pluralistic Society*, 111.
14. Wade Pickren, "Fifty Years On: Brown v. Board of Education and American Psychology, 1954-2004: An Introduction", 493-494.

schools is unconstitutional. Some progress has been made in improving racial disparities, but it has been slow, uneven, and incomplete.[15]) It is time for education in this country to change radically and this should begin with teachers forming a new attitude.

The teacher's attitude must be taught, and they must undergo training for this positive change to occur. Multiple Intelligences Theory should be implemented. We can let the students know that the curriculum revolves around them learning concepts and that it builds on every child's strengths; however, it is critical that the teacher demonstrates that they care. An appreciative, respectful, and caring environment will filter down to every child in the classroom.

Resources for Each Student

Stull and Wang[16] compared school achievement levels based on their percentage of minority students. The study investigated school organizational factors and teacher practices as they impact minority and non-minority achievement levels. The study indicated that the common characteristics of schools that predominately serve minority populations were larger class sizes, more special education classes, greater student mobility, more poor children, lower per pupil expenditures, and more frequent use of tracks or ability groups.

As teachers connect with parents, they may find that the parents have family members or friends who can offer an educational opportunity to the students. Teachers should welcome these friends into the classroom to share their expertise. The school's wider community could offer certain academic interests, such as a food store, a bank, or a library. The teacher should make enquiries at various places of businesses to see how they can become part of the classroom activities. Students learning about real life experiences in the community can provide valuable life lessons. The bank experience could start to teach students how to save money, while the grocery store can teach them about food and the importance of good nutrition in their growth and development. Teachers should try to make sure the businesses reflect the students' interests, as well as introducing them to people from other cultures. It is necessary to have appropriate materials for activities and

---

15. Spector, Carrie, "School Poverty—Not Racial Composition—Limits Educational Opportunity, According to New Research from Stanford".
16. Judith Stull and May Wang. "The Determinants of Achievement: Minority Students Compared to on-Minority Students".

projects. Sometimes, businesses many discard things that can be useful in the classroom. Also, there are organizations that may have free materials for educators. It is important for teachers to enquire about this so that the classroom can have the required materials to implement and complete activities and projects.

Lastly, technology is essential. Technology has so many virtual activities which can be a valuable resource for students and educators. What students cannot experience in real time, technology will allow through virtual trips. It is important to make sure that there are appropriate and updated computers and age-appropriate software for the children in the classroom. Every student from third grade and above should have access to a computer or iPad at home. Technology is appropriate for meeting the needs of students because of the varied educational software that is developmentally appropriate for differentiation in teaching the skills and concepts to meet the learning styles of each student.

Chapter Summary

The appreciation and respect that the teacher demonstrates in the classroom will filter through to the students. The teacher sets the tone of the classroom by modeling appropriate verbal and non-verbal behavior. The teacher should intentionally allow each child to be themselves and should ensure that the students always know the expectations in the classroom. The teacher can allow the students to develop the rules in the classroom. These classroom rules must be written in positive terms and limited to five rules at most. Since the students developed the rules, they will be able to remember them and remind their classmates when they are not abiding by them. This can be helpful to the teachers because the students will be practicing peer intervention. In addition, students are more likely to follow and remember rules that they have developed and implemented.

Teachers must be aware that one test is insufficient to measure a student's performance. Students have different learning styles. Students may be visual, auditory, or kinesthetic learners, or even have a combination of different learning styles. Therefore, it is necessary to have various assessments to ensure an accurate evaluation of a student's academic performance. This will also help to meet the students' expectations and facilitate positive outcomes.

The key resource for schools is the parent/family and developing the necessary bond between parent, child, and teacher. This bond makes school an extension of the child's home. Parents will feel that their involvement is important in helping their child to meet academic goals. The teacher needs to inform parents how they can reinforce their child's skills daily, and that education does not stop in the classroom but extends into the home. Academic challenges and rewards are not just the teacher's responsibilities but belong to the whole triad: parent, child, and teacher. This triad will build bridges, resolve problems, and create solutions for all the involved participants.

References

Brenchley, Cameron. "Equity and Excellence Commission Delivers Report to Secretary Duncan" *HomeRoom* (blog). U.S. Department of Education, February 20, 2013. https:// https://blog.ed.gov/2013/02/equity-and-excellence-commission-delivers-report-to-secretary-duncan/.

Cherry, Kendra. "Howard Gardner's Theory of Multiple Intelligences" July 17, 2019. https://www.verywellmind.com/gardners-theory-of-multiple-intelligences-2795161.

National Resource Centre for Health and Safety in Child Care, "Daily Health Checks". October 20, 2005. http://nrc.uchsc.edu/TIPS/heathchecks.htm.

Gollick, Donna, and Philip Chinn. *Multicultural Education in a Pluralistic Society,* Upper Saddle River: Pearson, 2009.

Grant, Kathy, and Julie Ray. *Home, School, and Community Collaboration.* Thousand Oaks: Sage, 2019.

Hale, Janice. *Learning while Black: Creating Educational Excellence for African American Children.* Baltimore: The Johns Hopkins University Press, 2001.

Irvine, Jacqueline Jordan, et al. *Comprehensive Urban Education.* Boston: Pearson Education, 2006.

Klein, Diane, and Deborah Chen. *Working with Children Culturally Diverse Backgrounds.* Albany: Delmar/Thomson Learning, 2001.

National Resource Center for Health and Safety in Childcare. "Caring for Our Children: National Health and Safety Performance Standards; Guidelines for Early Care and Education Programs (*CFOC*)". https://static.virtuallabschool.org.

Meier, Deborah, and Matthew Knoester. *Beyond Testing: Seven Assessments of Students and Schools.* New York: Teachers College Press, 2017.

Melser, Nancy. "Ain't Nothin' Like the Real Thing: Preparing Teachers in an Urban Environment". *Childhood Education* 82, no. 5 (2006): 228-231.

National Resource Centre for Health & Safety in Child Care. https://static.virtualabschool.org.

Pickren, Wade. "Fifty Years On: Brown v. Board of Education and American Psychology, 1954-2004: An Introduction", *American Psychologist 59,* no. 6, 2004: 493-494. https://doi.org/10.1037/0003-066X.59.6.493.

Richards, Delia. "The Integration of the Multiple Intelligence Theory into the Early Childhood Curriculum". *American Journal of Educational Research* 4, no.15, (2016): 1096-1099.

Saunders, Marisa, Jorge Ruiz De Valasco, and Jeannie Oakes, "Introduction". In *Learning Time in Pursuit of Educational Equity*, edited by Marisa Saunders, Jorge Ruiz De Valasco, and Jeannie Oakes, 3-5. Cambridge: Harvard Education Press, 2017.

Stull Judith and May Wang. "The Determinants of Achievement: Minority Students Compared to on-Minority Students". Paper presented at the annual meeting of the American Educational Research Association, Seattle, WA, 2001.

U.S. Department of Education. *For Each and Every Child. A Strategy for Education Equity and Excellence.* Washington: Office of Elementary and Secondary Education, February 2013.

CHAPTER 3

APPRECIATING STUDENTS' CULTURES

The third core value represented in the TEACHER acrostic is *Appreciating Students' Cultures*. The Webster Dictionary defines "appreciation" as the recognition and enjoyment of someone or something's good qualities. Some additional synonyms that also help us to define "appreciation" are admiration, cherishing, and valuing. The idea of being appreciated will make any child feel valued and respected. Teachers should think about appreciation in terms of their students; therefore, teachers should consider each student's unique characteristics and demonstrate to each one how they are important to the make-up of the classroom environment. Teachers can also address the following questions to enhance every students' self-esteem and the self-concept:

- How can teachers demonstrate appreciation for the students in the classroom?
- How should teachers manage the most difficult personality in the classroom?
- What is the relationship between appreciation and self-concept?
- Are there any specific activities that can demonstrate appreciation?

Demonstrating an Appreciation for the Students' Cultures

Sometimes students are overcome by the many functions that they endure in the classroom and there is always one student that will attempt to make life in the classroom more difficult than is necessary. Teachers must develop solutions that will curtail these situations. For example, students may lack the proper etiquette, but teachers may also assume that the students should know better because saying, "excuse me," "please," and "thank you" are common knowledge. Some students may use inappropriate language or try to bully special needs students or those who simply lack confidence in their own abilities. Other students may be determined to not follow the rules that have been developed and implemented by the students in the classroom.

Maniates, Doerr, and Golden reported that "if the teacher gets to know children personally, they can communicate their unequivocal belief in each student."[1] By trying to uncover every child's strengths, the teacher can find unrecognized abilities and underdeveloped potential to build upon.

The teacher must analyze every student's "All About Me" profiles to see what makes each one happy and to identify all of their different strengths. This will assist the teacher in developing a list of "how to" demonstrate their appreciation for each child. Another critical aspect of analyzing appreciation techniques for each student is the observation assessment technique (Template 7: Observation Tools). When the teacher spends time every day in the classroom analyzing the students' behavior, they will be amazed at what can be learned that would not ordinarily be noticed.

The teacher should spend time observing their students for at least one hour per day. This is enough time to give them a different outlook on each student. Observation is just watching without giving any specific assignment. It can be done during different times of day such as group time, individual lesson time, or free time/recess. It is ideal to observe the students at different times to see how they behave in different situations and how they interact with different peer groups. The teacher will learn about the students' interests and how the students get along with their peers and which groups of students work best in cooperative activities.

"Teachers and program leaders use observation protocols and checklists, as well as ongoing curriculum documentation strategies (such as audio-recording, children's conversations, and photography) to reflect on what children are learning".[2] For example, if a teacher observed that two students enjoy working together and that they questioned each other appropriately regarding information they have learned, the teacher could pair them for specific assignments. In contrast, the teacher would not put two students together if observations indicated that they were always in conflict. Observing students may also identify student leaders, shy and alone students, and outgoing and independent students. These kinds of observations can be useful when determining seating arrangements, identifying interactive groups, and selecting students for specific tasks.

1. Helen Maniates, Betty Doerr, and Margaret Golden, *Teacher Our Children Well: Essential Strategies for the Urban Classroom*, 8.
2. Louise Derman-Sparks, Debbie Lee Keenan, and John Nimmo, *Leading Anti-Bias Early Childhood Program: A Guide for Change*, 141.

Once teachers have observed the students in different classroom situations, they can be intentional when demonstrating appreciation for each student. The teacher must be sincere about valuing any contributions that the student brings to the classroom. For example, students who are well mannered, considerate of others, and attempt to follow directions and do the right thing should always be complimented. There are different ways to indicate to students that they are being appreciated. The teacher can say "that was very nice of you to hold the door (child's name), thank you," or "I like the way you always help your friends when they need assistance with an assignment." It is meaningful to the student when a teacher acknowledges that they are exhibiting their best behavior.

Robles de Melendez and Beck[3] define the following: "behaviors are actions exhibited by individuals in response to certain situations or stimuli".[4] Attitudes are the dispositions people have toward others and to circumstances that guide their overt and covert behavior. The attitudes and behaviors of both adults and children convey messages to children that help them to construct their own responses and ideas. This builds the foundation for some of the attitudes and behaviors related to multicultural education such as acceptance, understanding, and tolerance of the cultural differences present in society and in the classroom. Teachers who recognize a student's positive behavior, set a positive tone for the classroom. A compliment or an acknowledgement lets the students know what constitutes positive behavior in the classroom.

In addition to daily verbal compliments to the students, teachers can also use awards, such as certificates of appreciations, that are distributed quarterly. Teachers should attempt to show appreciation to all students. It may be necessary to help some students achieve appreciation awards by giving them cues to encourage them to accomplish positive tasks for others. Sometimes the teacher can say to a student, "please can you collect the papers?" or "please can you make sure all the students have a pencil?" Allowing students to achieve small tasks encourages them to recognize that they can also be appreciated.

If the classroom environment is the foundation for valuing each student, the atmosphere for demonstrating appreciation for one another is in place.

---

3. Wilma Robles de Melendez and Verna Beck, *Teaching Young Children in Multicultural Classrooms: Issues, Concepts, and Strategies*, 340.
4. Wilma Robles de Melendez and Verna Beck, *Teaching Young Children in Multicultural Classrooms*, 340.

Espinosa[5] demonstrated that culturally responsive classrooms have teachers who specifically acknowledge both the presence of culturally and linguistically diverse students and the need for these students to feel comfortable, accepted, safe, and intellectually engaged. The teacher should recognize the strengths and needs of each child and develop appropriate instructional approaches. As a result, the teacher will recognize the unique characteristics of every student while setting common goals. Of course, this starts with the teacher modeling positive behavior so that students realize that they will be valued and appreciated for the consideration that they show to each other. When a student knows that they are appreciated, it filters into their daily activities. Once students know they are valued, they will want to reach their optimal potential in their studies and behavior. The idea of being valued and appreciated filters through to all activities including their social development. "The process of social transformation requires a special setting conducive to the children's dreaming, fantasizing, building skills, and socialization."[6]

Teachers should use verbal compliments, extrinsic rewards, and sharing the idea of appreciation with other students in the classroom are also important tools. In addition, one assignment that teachers can give to students is for everyone to write down what they appreciate about another student. Depending on the grade level, students can write an appreciation sentence or several adjectives about another student. The teacher must make sure that every student's name has been passed out. This is a great assignment to teach students to appreciate and value one another.

In addition, complimenting a child with positive feedback can increase positive behavior. For example, saying, "Thank you, Robert, for putting all the blocks away. Our classroom is organized now because of your help," demonstrates how helpful the child has been and acknowledges how important the child is in the organization of the classroom. This simple acknowledgement is giving respect to the child and assisting in building the child's self-concept. At the same time, teachers are demonstrating their expectation of classroom behavior.

Children want to please their teacher. When the teacher gives positive feedback and acknowledgements, they are modeling the types of behaviors that are expected in the classroom. It is necessary for the teacher to set the

5. Linda Espinosa, *Getting It Right for Young Children from Diverse Backgrounds*, 84.
6. Wilma Robles de Melendez and Verna Beck, *Teaching Young Children in Multicultural Classrooms: Issues, Concepts, and Strategies*, 341.

tone of the classroom environment. The teacher should allow the students to assist in developing and implementing five rules, they will form the foundation for how the classroom operates. Five rules or less are suggested because you want the students to remember and abide by the rules. The teacher will manage the classroom by consistently applying the established rules, providing tasks and activities for all students, and acknowledging positive behavior. This demonstration makes negative behavior feel out of place in the classroom because little attention is given to behaviors that do not show positive outcomes.

Klein and Chen[7] give the following eight suggestions for dealing with children's behavior and social interactions:

- "Interact with children who need one-on-one attention in small groups.
- Give children a choice if they do not express a preference or initiate an activity.
- Do not force children to make eye contact.
- Do not pressure children to talk.
- Provide many alternative means of expression through art, puppets, music, and signing.
- If the students use the teacher's first name, they should say, for example, "Miss Tanya" to demonstrate respect, which is important in many families.[8]
- For young children who have not yet been separated from their mothers, encourage their mothers to stay for the first part of the class. Make sure every mother says goodbye to their child.
- Provide opportunities for self-direction until children are used to the schedule and routine. If a child does not respond to positive discipline use firm commands, at least initially. Gradually help the child comply with less direct forms of instruction."

If these suggestions are followed, children will realize that a positive environment is built on appropriate behaviour that results in kindness and respect for all the students. The National Association for the Education of Young Children[9] maintained that space in the early childhood classroom

---

7. Diane Klein and Deborah Chen, *Working with Children Culturally Diverse Backgrounds*, 118-119.
8. Stacey York, *Roots and Wings: Affirming Culture in Early Childhood Programs*.
9 National Association for the Education of Young Children (NAEYC), *Accreditation Criteria for Programs Serving Children from Birth Through Age 8*,

should be distributed into learning or interest areas, centers, or stations. Certain materials should be stored in these areas.[10] Also, Roble de Melendez and Beck[11] suggested that the instructional resources in the learning centers should reflect the characteristics of the children, their families, and the community. This is accomplished by including a variety of non-biased, non-sexist, and multicultural materials.

Fergus, Noguera, and Martin[12] noted that Black and Latino boys, among the most vulnerable populations in our schools, face persistent and devastating disparities in achievement compared to their White counterparts. These researchers suggested that many educators addressed the needs of boys of color by using "hooks" in the curriculum. These hooks are described as strategies that allow the young men to see themselves in the curriculum; other educators have described these strategies as real-world applications. These researchers observed the instructional strategies in seven all-male schools that serviced primarily low-income Black and Latino families; they concluded that the students' level of proficiency varied and that it was often not clear whether the students were being pushed academically. The grade levels of the schools varied from 4th–12th grade.

Appreciation and Self-Concept

Self-concept is how students feels about themselves. Diehl and Hay[13] stated that self-concept refers to the clarity, confidence, and consistency of an individual's definitions of themselves. Another definition of self-concept is how someone thinks about, evaluates, or perceives themselves (simplypsychology.org). Self-concept is malleable when people are younger and still going through the process of self-discovery and the formation of self-identity (verywellmind.com). Gestwicki[14] emphasizes that children need to know that their teacher believes they are capable of

cited by Wilma Robles de Melendez and Verna Beck, *Teaching Young Children in Multicultural Classrooms: Issues*, 343.
10. JoAnn Brewer, *Introduction to Early Childhood Education: Preschool Through the Primary Grades*, 99.
11. Wilma Roble de Melendez and Verna Beck, *Teaching Young Children in Multicultural Classrooms*, 269.
12. Edward Fergus, Pedro Noguera, and Margary Martin, *Schooling for Resilience. Improving the Life Trajectory of Black and Latino Boys*, 1.
13. Manfred Diehl and Elizabeth Hay, "Self-Concept Differentiation and Self-Concept Clarity Across Adulthood: Associations with Age and Psychological Well", 125-132.
14. Carol Gestwicki, *Home, School, and Community Relations.*

learning, no matter their social class, ethnic background, or gender. Children must be treated with equal and positive respect and responsiveness. The teacher must remember that the way others respond to children helps to form their self-concept, and that children will behave according to the image of themselves that they perceive others hold.

Self-concept should be considered when planning the curriculum.[15] Once students are confident of who they are, the ability to combat any obstacles in the learning process will be easier to overcome. Positive self-concept will trickle into behavior, learning, and peer/teacher relationships. Students who feel good about themselves will easily respect others since they will want to please the teacher and will feel confident that they can be the best student possible.

When students are being taught to have a positive self-concept, it is necessary for teachers to examine their own biases through self-reflection to make sure they are practicing equity, inclusion, and respect for every student. Klein and Chen[16] noted that one of the goals for a multicultural early childhood education program is to develop a positive self-concept in those children most affected by racism.

Teachers should educate themselves on their students' respective cultures. The best way to learn about culture is from the students' parents and families. Teachers should make sure they include families when introducing students' cultural experience to the other students. Using a map or a globe to demonstrate the origins of the various students is helpful. Learning about their food, music, clothes, and other cultural aspects is also important. However, the curriculum should include these cultural aspects on a daily basis and not be limited to a singular cultural day to celebrate, for instance, Black, Native American, or Latino history. Derman-Sparks[17] refers to a singular cultural day, week, or month celebration as a "tourist curriculum." Instead, culture should be a daily part of the curriculum and this should begin with the cultures of the children in the classroom.

Often teachers do not focus on self-concept or the significance of diversity in the classroom. As a result, some students will feel devalued and believe that they do have any contributions to share because their experiences are not the same as the other students' experiences. This could be because the

---

15. James Beane, *Self-Concept and Self-Esteem as Curriculum Issues*, 504-506.
16. Diane Klein and Deborah Chen, *Working with Children Culturally Diverse Backgrounds*, 34.
17. Louise Derman-Sparks, "Children-Socioeconomic Class and Equity," 50-53.

students are from a different country, speak a different language, eat different kinds of food, listen to different music, or celebrate different holidays. This is what is called a different cultural experience. When cultural experiences and differences are not shared or discussed, the students may think that differences are negative or that their experiences are not worth being shared. Therefore, it is essential to focus on inclusion and the different cultural experiences when teaching and learning to demonstrate equity, respect, and appreciation for the diverse students in the classroom.

Howe and Lisi[18] proposed that two areas of responsibility include being culturally responsive and preparing all students for a multicultural society. This involves using the students' cultural backgrounds within the curriculum and moving all students from monocultural knowledge and skills to multicultural ones. In addition, Zerchner[19] suggested that this multicultural experience is a key to ensuring that all students achieve high levels of education.

Sometimes, students treat each other differently because of the way they look or because their different cultural experiences prevent them from relating to others. This may result in students being unkind or feeling uncomfortable among their peers. Demonstrating the importance of every student in the classroom, regardless of their cultural background allows them to appreciate and respect one another. The classroom environment must encourage contributions made by every student and include learning how people can be different and similar at the same time. Students must have an opportunity to experience their classmates' cultures by sharing activities and discussing their experiences.

The teacher can influence the development of a positive self-concept by creating opportunities for diverse students that will impact their beliefs about who they are, what they can accomplish, and what the future has in store for them. Two quotations sum this up: "The sky is the limit" and "You can be whatever you want to be." Other impactful quotations include: "There is no such word as "can't" and "There are no stupid questions apart from the one that is not asked." These quotations are affirmations and are a foundation to building and developing a positive self-concept.

The development of a positive self-concept is the beginning of feeling good about oneself, which can then develop into a student's worthwhile connection

---

18. William Howe and Penelope Lisi, *Becoming a Multicultural Educator,* 24.
19. Kenneth Zerchner, "Educating Teachers to Close the Gap: Issues of Pedagogy, Knowledge and Teacher Preparation".

with their diverse classmates. Before someone can treat others appropriately, they must feel good about themselves. Kopetz, Lease, and Warren-King stated "low self-esteem likely leads to behaviour problems that may lead to violent or criminal activities."[20]

Teachers are role models for their students. Teachers must be aware of how they treat every student, and they must be able to assure that equity is practiced in all arenas of their classroom. Klein and Chen[21] cited that what young children learn in an early childhood setting is influenced by their teacher's expectations. It is important that the teacher is aware of unconscious preconceptions and negative stereotypes that may influence their expectation of a child and their interpretation of the child's behavior.

The teacher should keep a record of which students are being called on to respond to answers. Keeping this record will assist the teacher to call on each student daily and ensure that everyone is playing an active role each day.

The teacher can make sure that positive verbal praise is given to every student daily. If it is difficult to give a student positive verbal praise, then the teacher can ask them to accomplish a task that requires a "thank you so much," after it has been completed. The teacher should always have positive compliments to give students, such as "your haircut looks nice" or "I like your new backpack." The more positive feedback you can give a student, the more comfortable the student will be in the classroom. Students want to please their teacher and helping the students feel good about themselves will translate into the students liking school, their teacher, and their classmates.

Specific Appreciation Activities

In the early childhood classroom, there are many activities that are assigned to the students that will install a positive self-concept. There is no reason why these activities cannot also be implemented in the upper grades. Some examples of activities include bringing family pictures into the classroom, writing about family members, listing the reasons for a favorite holiday, and describing an exciting trip or experience. Other activities include discussing favorite foods, making a collective recipe book of each student's tastiest

---

20. Patricia Kopetz, Anthony Lease, and Bonnie Warren-Kring, *Comprehensive Urban Education,* 195.
21. Diane Klein and Deborah Chen, *Working with Children Culturally Diverse Backgrounds*, 126-127.

meal, drawing a portrait of themselves, writing about their own strengths, describing their hobbies with their classmates, and sharing what they enjoy doing during their free time.

Teachers must make sure that the activities they use are inclusive. For example, when discussing travel always have a choice of another activity in the event a student has not travelled anywhere else. Assigning an activity entitled "All About Me" is a great way for students to learn about themselves; it also gives the teacher another opportunity to learn about their students and to provide new experiences for them. When students are given appropriate choices for activities, they feel good about themselves and their experiences. Researchers have synthesized elements from both the structural (reducing individuals to passive objects of larger forces) and culturalists (the "blame the victim" perspective) points of view to incorporate a greater focus on the importance of individual choice and agency.[22]

Some activities that students can easily talk about are their favorite food, their favorite subject in school, their best friend, their favorite holiday, their favorite season, and a place in their city or close by that they would love to visit. These topics are inclusive, and students do not have to feel bad because they, unlike a classmate, never went to Disney World or abroad. These types of activities not only value the individual student in the classroom, but they teach the other students that diversity is valued, individuals are valued, and that every voice is important and beneficial to the learning experience. They also show that they are a part of the whole teaching and learning experience.

Although teachers do not explicitly discuss values, inclusion, or equity, they are implied from the activities and the teaching and learning experiences that are implemented throughout the classroom. The saying, "actions speak louder than words" is important here. Instead of making diversity a problem that the teacher does not know how to manage, the suggested experiences and activities will build the foundation for including diverse students. As a result, students will excel because they feel included and valued. Also, the teacher will have demonstrated that no experience is better than another. All students bring their own knowledge to the classroom and all students can learn from each other. When a student knows that they are critical to ensuring the whole learning process is implemented, they feel a part of it.

Making each student feel good about who they are is necessary to helping them reach their maximum potential. It is like a big puzzle where every

---

22. Michelle Fine, *Framing Dropouts: Notes on The Politics of an Urban Public High School*, 1991.

student has a piece of the puzzle that will make the learning process complete. This process will be effective when every puzzle piece has been fitted in the appropriate place. Completing this puzzle with a piece of the puzzle that represents each child in the classroom can be shared with the students, as it lets them know that every student is valued and is critical to completing a learning process that will benefit the entire class.

Chapter Summary

The teacher should analyze the "All About Me" profile for each child and use it to identify their students' strengths and interests. In addition, observing students daily and taking notes to analyze and reflect on will help the teacher to recognize them as individuals. Being appreciated will make any child feel valued and respected.

Acknowledging a student's good behavior is important for developing a positive classroom environment. Students will want to meet their optimum potential if they know they are being valued and respected. The teacher can give verbal compliments and extrinsic rewards, such as certificates. The foundation of the classroom is the development and implementation of its five rules. The teacher should attempt to support each student in developing their self-concept.

Teachers should analyze their own biases and self-reflect to make sure they are practicing equity, inclusion, and respect for each child. Teachers should learn about the cultures of the students in their classroom. Parents and families can be the best method for teachers to learn about their students' cultures. Teachers should implement different cultural aspects into the curriculum every day.

Teachers must give positive feedback to their students and model positive behavior as the foundation for growth and development both in and outside the classroom. Teachers should make appropriate choices when giving students activities so that all students are included in the lesson. The idea is to make each child feel valued, respected, and appreciated.

References

Beane, James. *Self-Concept and Self-Esteem as Curriculum Issues.* Alexandria: Association for Supervision and Curriculum Development, 1982.

Brewer, JoAnn. *Introduction to Early Childhood Education. Preschool Through the Primary Grades.* Boston: Allyn and Bacon, 1992.

Derman-Sparks, Louise, "Children-Socioeconomic Class and Equity". *Young Children* 64, no. 3 (2009): 50-53.

Derman-Sparks, Louise, Debbie Lee Keenan, and John Nimmo. *Leading Anti-Bias Early Childhood Program: A Guide for Change.* New York: Teachers College Press and Washington: NAEYC, 2015.

Diehl, Manfred, and Elizabeth Hay. "Self-Concept Differentiation and Self-Concept Clarity Across Adulthood: Associations with Age and Psychological Well". *The International Journal of Aging and Human Development* 73, no. 2 (2011):125-152.

Espinosa, Linda. (2015). *Getting It Right for Young Children from Diverse Backgrounds.* Upper Saddle River: Pearson, 2015.

Fergus, Edward, Pedro Noguera, and Margary Martin. *Schooling for Resilience. Improving the Life Trajectory of Black and Latino Boys.* Cambridge: Harvard Education Press, 2014.

Fine, Michelle. *Framing Dropouts: Notes on The Politics of an Urban Public High School.* Albany: State University of New York Press, 1991.

Howe, William, and Penelope Lisi. *Becoming a Multicultural Educator: Developing Awareness, Gaining Skills and Taking Action.* Oakland: Sage, 2020.

Klein, Diane, and Deborah Chen. *Working with Children Culturally Diverse Backgrounds.* Albany: Delmar/Thomson Learning, 2001, 118-119.

Kopetz, Patricia, Anthony Lease, and Bonnie Warren-Kring. *Comprehensive Urban Education.* Boston: Pearson, 2006.

Maniates, Helen, Betty Doerr and Margaret Golden. *Teacher Our Children Well: Essential Strategies for the Urban Classroom.* Portsmouth, NH: Heinemann, 2001.

National Association for the Education of Young Children (NAEYC). *Accreditation Criteria for Programs Serving Children from Birth Through Age 8.* Washington: NAEYC, 1991.

Robles de Melendez, Wilma, and Verna Beck. *Teaching Young Children in Multicultural Classrooms: Issues, Concepts, and Strategies.* Albany: Delmar/Thomson Learning, 2007.

York, Stacey. *Roots and Wings: Affirming Culture in Early Childhood Programs.* St. Paul: Redleaf Press, 1991.

Zerchner, Kenneth. "Educating Teachers to Close the Gap: Issues of Pedagogy, Knowledge and Teacher Preparation." In *Closing the Achievement Gap: A Vision to Guide Changes in Beliefs and Practice,* edited by Belinda Williams, 39-52. Philadelphia, PA: Research for Better Schools, 1995.

CHAPTER 4

COMMUNICATING WITH STUDENTS

The fourth core value represented in the TEACHER acrostic is *Communicating with Students*. Every idea or concept that is used in the classroom must be intentional because, although teachers want to build on the child's strengths, they must be aware of the child's weaknesses in order to improve or eliminate them. The teacher's goal is to build a well-rounded student who is fully developed socially, emotionally, physically, cognitively, and intellectually. These domains are critical in reaching the student's optimal potential. To address these domains, the teacher must answer the following fundamental questions:

- How does the teacher support, recognize, and implement differentiated instruction?
- How do the student and teacher communicate?
- How do the teacher and the parents/family communicate?
- What effect does the teacher's attitude have on student learning?

Supporting Differentiated Instruction

Gay[1] and Sheets[2] indicated that culture impacts what happens in the classroom on a daily basis. School is a student's work. The teacher should want to make the classroom environment stimulating, innovative, and interesting. The teacher should know their students' interests, the environment that they all come from, and recognize that their first teachers are their parents or caregivers. The teacher must refer to the student profiles that were discussed in Chapter 2 and which were completed at the beginning of the school year.

The teacher should refer to the student profiles as data to enable them to develop a classroom environment that will be interesting to all their students

---

1. Geneva Gay, *Culturally Responsive Teaching: Theory, Research, and Practice*, 50.
2. Rosa Hernandez Sheets, *Diversity Pedagogy: Examining the Role of Culture in the Teaching Learning Process*, 50.

and, at the same time, meet their individual needs. For example, if a teacher knows that a favorite food for many of the children in the classroom is pizza, they can prepare pizza together for a science/cooking experience that uses the language experience chart with a recipe including pictures and step-by-step directions. In addition, the teacher could have each child make a paper pizza for math (Template 9: Teaching Fractions with Pizza). If ice cream was a favorite dessert, then the teacher could make a graph demonstrating how many students like the different flavors (Template 10: What is your Favorite Flavor of Ice Cream?). On that day, a special treat could be provided by serving ice cream for a dessert or snack in the classroom. These examples demonstrate how teachers can implement their students' interests into the various curriculum domains. This can also provide an opportunity for each student to share their feelings as well as to retell or discuss their experiences while the teacher writes their reflections on a chart during the conclusion of the activity.

The goal of personalizing the curriculum and making learning fun will be achieved when the teacher incorporates their students' interests as a part of teaching and learning. Invariably, the students will then become more excited about and engaged with learning.

Although some of the concepts that have been discussed may initially be difficult for certain students, they will become less challenging because of the personalization that has been demonstrated throughout the curriculum. This type of integration makes learning concepts exciting and fun. Instead of students focusing on what they do not know or like, the teacher can use the students' interests and likes to introduce and teach challenging concepts. Gollnick and Chinn[3] discussed culturally responsive teaching encourages student participation, critical analysis, and action. Classroom projects should focus on areas of interest to the students and the communities in which they live."

The three learning styles—visual, auditory, and tactile—form the ways that students learn (Template 11: Learning Styles). A description of a visual learner is someone who learns best through seeing. Wall charts and posters are incredibly supportive for this type of learner. An auditory learner learns best through hearing. Verbalizing instructions can be helpful for this learner. Tactile learners learn best by touching. This learner benefits from hands-on activities. The teacher should introduce concepts in all three ways. This idea

---

3. Donna Gollnick and Philip Chinn, *Multicultural Education in a Pluralistic Society*, 386.

ensures that the teacher has encompassed the diverse learning styles of all the students in the classroom.

In addition, integrating Howard Gardner's Multiple Intelligences Theory accommodates these different learning styles (Template 12: Multiple Intelligences). According to Webster's dictionary, intelligence can be defined as the ability to acquire and apply information to solve problems. Gardner's theory of multiple intelligences outlines distinct areas of intellect. His theory can be integrated into the curriculum, as well as used for self-reflection and determining one's strengths. Gardner's theory includes nine areas of intelligences.[4] The first area of intelligence, linguistic, involves language. The second area of intelligence, logical-mathematical, involves reasoning, objects, and mathematical problems. The third area of intelligence, musical, musical performance and composition. The fourth area of intelligence, spatial, involves visualization. The fifth area of intelligence, bodily-kinesthetic, involves movement. The sixth area of intelligence, intrapersonal, involves self-awareness. The seventh area of intelligence, interpersonal, involves social skills. The eighth area of intelligence, naturalist, involves the human ability to discriminate among living things. The ninth area of intelligence, existential, involves sensitivity and the capacity to tackle deep questions about human existence.[5] Reviewing each student's data from the profile sheets, incorporating each child's interest in the curriculum, and integrating Multiple Intelligences Theory in the curriculum can minimize the students' challenges. If a challenge has been affected by the impact of positive influences, then the students will be able to overcome the challenge more easily within this nurturing environment.

Two-Way Communication—Teacher and Student

Boutte[6] suggests that the communication styles of different cultures may not be the norm for all students. Boutte also noted that the problems that many children face inside and outside classrooms (racism, poverty, language differences, and cultural barriers) are not adequately acknowledged and addressed in most schools. As a result, schools continue to experience low achievement and high dropout rates among certain groups.

---

4. Thomas Armstrong, *Multiple Intelligences in the Classroom*, 1-2.
5. Thomas Armstrong, *Multiple Intelligences in the Classroom*, 1-2.
6. Gloria Boutte, *Multicultural Education: Raising Consciousness*, 129.

When a student has bonded with their teacher, the learning environment becomes an ideal situation for both of them. Upon arrival at school, a teacher's goal should be to communicate with each child every single morning and to ensure that every student has a great day in the classroom. The teacher should want to know whether a child has had a difficult previous evening as this gives an indication of the child's mental or emotional status. It also enables teachers to determine if any planned activities should be altered or if any additional discussions with the child are needed during the day. Samples of additional discussion topics may include talking about a child's lost pet or the weather, such as a snow or rainstorm event the prior evening. Other topics include whether the student or family member was transported to the emergency ward at the hospital, if a parent has returned home from the military, or if there was a visit to a parent's job. Lack of dinner, possibly no breakfast in the morning, or gunshots in their neighborhood must be recognized once the student arrives at school so that they are exposed to a fun classroom that is welcoming and positive, while offering a rewarding learning activity. The student should know that they will be cared for in a happy and safe environment conducive to effective teaching. This knowledge will have a positive impact on the students' growth and development.

As well as greeting their students in the morning and asking how they are feeling, the teacher should also ensure that each child shares a reflection of their current day. A poem by author and poet Joshua Dickerson[7] reminds teachers that they do not know what their students have encountered before they get to school. This poem is called "Cause I Ain't Got a Pencil."

---

7. Joshua Dickerson

Cause I Ain't Got a Pencil

by Joshua T. Dickerson

I woke myself up
Because we ain't got an alarm clock
Dug in the dirty clothes basket,
Cause ain't nobody washed my uniform
Brushed my hair and teeth in the dark,
Cause the lights ain't on
Even got my baby sister ready,
Cause my mama wasn't home.
Got us both to school on time,
To eat us a good breakfast.
Then when I got to class the teacher fussed
Cause I ain't got a pencil.

When the student leaves for home in the afternoon, the teacher should always wish the student a good evening and remind them to complete homework assignments or projects that are due the next day. The teacher should also end the day with a positive quote or find a moment to have afternoon reflections. During this time, the students can share how their day went including what they enjoyed and what they would like to change.

The teacher should also provide the student with verbal words of encouragement about accomplishments or improvements made during the day. Closing the day with these positive affirmations may help students' evening at home to become inspirational and it also provides them with positive feedback to share with their parents/families. If any disappointment or challenges occurred during the day, then the student group can collectively come up with solutions to the issue.

A whole afternoon reflection, which demonstrates the importance of daily reflection, gives students time to help each other resolve issues. Students will learn that reflection can become a way to solve situations and to prepare one's self to endure the next challenge. Reflecting also demonstrates to students that their peers are also a support group. Each day, students can reflect on and discuss their likes and dislikes, which encourages them to look forward to the next school day. To emphasize the lesson, the teacher may encourage each student to develop a reflection journal for this activity. Daily learning experience of reflection can also be in the form of written or pictorial activities. This allows the student's experiences to be captured and kept as a record of their experiences throughout the school year. The teacher should be the one who decides whether the journal should be shared.

Teacher and Parents/Family Communication

Cooper[8] provides five steps to make parents the teacher's allies. The teacher must ensure that the following steps are accomplished at the beginning of the school year:

1. Prepare a short introduction statement, which should be carried home and returned with the parent's signature.
2. Send home disciplinary and homework policies that are to be signed and returned.
3. Obtain parents and guardians' home, work, and cell telephone numbers on the first day.
4. Call all parents at the beginning of the year, especially if a student is falling behind or if there is a behaviour problem.
5. Insist on a visit from the parents if any problem persists.

Always stress "WE" when communicating with parents. This enforces the notion that the teacher and the parent will work together on behalf of the child. It would be great if every student could have a parent/family representative when special events happen in the classroom, such as Grandparent's Day, Father's Breakfast, or Mother's Day luncheon. This is a good time to call on volunteers or community helpers if some students will not have anyone to accompany them during one of these activities. It makes students happier and they feel a part of things when they have someone there for them.

Teachers should be mindful that parents are the students' first teacher, and the teacher should want them to be included in classroom activities. The teacher, child, and family/parents all working together on behalf of the child will encourage and support the child's ability to learn. When a bond has

---

8. Ryan Cooper, *Those Who Can, Teach*, 485-486.

been created and all are viewed as school partners, a smooth academic transition can be created. Douglas[9] discussed how one educator created a welcoming family space at her program and changed the morning drop-off protocols to allow parents to come into the building and have an opportunity to speak with teachers.

Teachers should make sure that the classroom is a place that parents are welcomed and, if there is a language barrier, the school should ensure that an interpreter is provided. Not all parents can attend meetings as there may be factors, such as work requirements or additional home childcare needs, that prohibit their attendance.

To address this, a volunteer system may be put in place by implementing a sign-up sheet delivered to each child's home. This sheet should include tasks that can be accomplished from their home. These activities could include making decorations, bringing artifacts to share in the classroom, making booklets, and making costumes for a program. The teacher should also call parents to remind them of a special school activity. Of course, teachers should supply parents/family with the necessary materials for the activities. When teachers can accommodate parents and include them in classroom activities, trust is created and respect is shown for the parent/family.

Kopetz, Lease, and Warren-Kring[10] expressed that teachers must be proactive in involving parents in their child's education. Teachers should not mistake a lack of involvement from parents to mean that they do not care. Urban parents, particularly the poor, care deeply about their children and recognize that education is important for them to optimally function in society. Teachers must convince parents of the importance of their role in their child's education. Researchers continue to state that it is the teacher's job to reach out to urban students and parents. The three necessary ingredients for teachers to incorporate daily in their rapport with students and parents include:

- understanding the condition under which the child lives,
- acquiring the skill and patience to provide instruction at each student's level, and
- providing a genuine demonstration of love for the children.

---

9. Anne Douglas, *Leading for Change in Early Care and Education*, 19.
10. Patricia Kopetz, Anthony Lease, and Bonnie Warren-Kring, *Comprehensive Urban Education*, 90.

Teachers who incorporate these three ingredients into their teaching will be surprised at the level of appreciation from parents and the extent to which students will crave learning. There is ample evidence that suggests that when parents are involved in their child's education, the child's academic achievement is positively affected.[11]

The Teacher's Attitude

"A person's attitudes, that is, his or her predispositions to act in a positive or negative way toward people, ideas, and events, are a fundamental dimension of that individual's personality".[12] Cooper describes four categories of attitude that affect teaching behavior:

- The teacher's attitude toward themself,
- The teacher's attitude toward children and the relationship they have with them,
- The teacher's attitude toward peers and the students' parents, and
- The teacher's attitude toward the subject matter.

Robles de Melendez and Beck[13] defined attitudes as the dispositions people have towards others and/or to a circumstance that guides their overt and covert behavior. According to Cooper,[14] the following skills for effective teaching would be effective if teachers practiced them for every child:

- asking different kinds of questions, each requiring different types of thought processes from the student;
- providing effective feedback;
- planning instruction and learning activities;
- diagnosing student needs and learning difficulties;
- varying the learning situation to keep the students involved;
- recognizing when students are paying attention and to use the information to vary behavior and, maybe, the direction of the lesson;
- using technological equipment, such as computers, to enhance student learning;
- assessing student learning; and

---

11. Jeremy Finn and Donald Rock, "Academic Success Among Students at Risk for School Failure", 221-234.
12. Ryan Cooper, *Those Who Can, Teach*, 171.
13. Wilma Robles de Melendez and Verna Beck, *Teaching Young Children in Multicultural Classrooms: Issues, Concepts, and Strategies*, 340.
14. Ryan Cooper, *Those Who Can, Teach*, 185.

- differentiating instruction based on the students' experiences, interests, and academic abilities.

Cooper[15] concluded that this list is far from complete but suggest that teachers need a wide repertoire of skills to work effectively with students from diverse backgrounds and different educational experiences.

The teacher's attitude is a critical component in creating change in the education process. Teachers must view themselves first and be honest about the biases that they may have regarding children, families, race, and culture. Teachers must appreciate and respect the different cultures represented in their classrooms. There may have been a time when teachers expressed a negative attitude towards students who were different or did not come from the same background as the teacher. Teachers can no longer possess the mindset that different is bad or better. Boutte[16] affirms that most educators believe that they provide equal opportunities for success for all children. However, a careful review of their attitudes and actions reveal that biases have crept into the classrooms unbeknown to the teachers.[17]

Cooper[18] stated that cultural pluralism is the notion of understanding and appreciating the cultural differences and languages among U.S. citizens. The idea is to create a sense of society's wholeness based on the unique strengths of each of its parts. Unfortunately, U.S. schools have often failed to support cultural pluralism. Traditionally, public schools have been run for the benefit of the dominant cultural group, thereby excluding minority groups from receiving the full range of benefits.

Students from another culture or background must be entitled to the same educational privileges as others in the classroom. As an example, this may be enforced by attaching a pin to each student's clothing saying that "attitude is everything." Every student is unique. In a family with children from the same biological parents, every child in that family is different, and so we know there are many differences in a classroom. It is important that teachers demonstrate positive attitudes towards every student in the classroom. When students are from different cultural or ethnic backgrounds, teachers need to go the extra mile and address the needs of all their students by acquiring cultural information about each one.

---

15. Ryan Cooper, *Those Who Can, Teach*, 185.
16. Gloria Boutte, *Multicultural Education: Raising Consciousness*, 88.
17. Boutte, *Multicultural Education: Raising Consciousness*, 96.
18. Ryan Cooper, *Those Who Can, Teach*, 61.

According to Maniates, Doerr, and Golden,[19] "one of the first elements in the formation of a climate for learning is one that seems to be the simplest––the teacher knows and develops a personal rapport with each child in the class."[20] Knowing their students' likes and dislikes enable the teacher to build concepts within the curriculum based on familiar and relatable things to them. The students will begin to trust and will develop a bond with the teacher when they recognize that the teacher is interested in them, is demonstrating that they care about their learning experience, and have their best interests at heart.

Teachers will need to make sure that all student jobs, such as line leader, passing out papers, taking attendance, and taking the lunch count to the office, are rotated so each student receives an opportunity to participate (Template 13: Job Chart). Paying daily compliments to students can be rewarding and helps to build a positive self-concept. Of course, the compliments must be sincere. All efforts that teachers make to develop a foundation for equity in the classroom must reflect genuine feelings. Students will know if teachers do not mean what they are doing or saying, and the results will not be positive from the student's perspective. Of course, when the teacher develops and builds equity in the classroom, an environment is created that will have valuable benefits for all involved. It will also provide a model of what is appropriate for the students.

Finding out about the many cultural differences and similarities can be a learning experience for the teacher and students. When teachers demonstrate that students and their cultures are important, it gives them a feeling of belonging and wanting to meet the learning objectives that the teacher has established. Kopetz, Lease, and Warren-Kring[21] suggested that, when teachers believe that marginalized students have the ability to succeed and hold them to high levels of academic achievement, these students will indeed succeed at high levels.

Chapter Summary

Teachers must be intentional and build on their students' strengths. Teachers need to personalize the curriculum by incorporating their students'

19. Helen Maniates, Betty Doerr, and Margaret Golden, *Teacher Our Children Well: Essential Strategies for the Urban Classroom*, 1.
20. Helen Maniates, Betty Doerr and Margaret Golden, *Teacher Our Children Well,* 1.
21. Patricia Kopetz, Anthony Lease, and Bonnie Warren-Kring, *Comprehensive Urban Education*, 230.

interests. The curriculum should incorporate the students' learning styles and Multiple Intelligences Theory to accommodate diverse learners. In addition, teachers should be aware of their students' weaknesses in order to improve and eliminate them. Researchers have suggested that culturally responsive teaching encourages student participation, critical analysis, and action.

It is important that teachers communicate with their students and parents. Daily communication with students will create a bond with the teacher. Teachers need to remember that parents are their students' first teachers; therefore, they should initiate contact and interact with parents to encourage their involvement in their child's schooling. Research has shown that parental involvement affects a child's academic achievement in a positive manner.

Teachers must go the extra mile for each child in order to build a positive rapport. Research has demonstrated that, when teachers believe that their students can succeed and hold them to high academic levels, academic performance is positively affected.

References

Armstrong, Thomas. *Multiple Intelligences in the Classroom*. Alexandria: Association for Supervision and Curriculum Development, 2000.
Bennett, Christine I. *Comprehensive Multicultural Education: Theory and Practice*, 7th ed. (Boston: Pearson, 2011).
Cooper, Ryan. *Those Who Can, Teach*. Boston: Wadsworth, 2010.
Douglas, Anne. *Leading for Change in Early Care and Education*. New York: Teacher's College Press, 2017.
Eliason, Claudia, & Loa Jenkins. *A Practical Guide to Early Childhood Education Curriculum*, 7th ed. New York: Merrill, 2002.
Finn, Jeremy, and Donald Rock. (1997). "Academic Success Among Students at Risk for School Failure". *Journal of Applied Psychology*, 82, no. 2 (1997): 221-234.
Gay, Geneva. *Culturally Responsive Teaching: Theory, Research, and Practice,* 2nd ed. New York: Teachers College Press, 2000.
Gollnick, Donna, and Philip Chinn. *Multicultural Education in a Pluralistic Society*. Upper Saddle River: Pearson, 2009.
Howe, William, and Penelope Lisi. *Becoming a Multicultural Educator: Developing Awareness, Gaining Skills and Taking Action*. Oakland: Sage, 2020.

Kopetz, Patricia, Anthony Lease, and Bonnie Warren-Kring. *Comprehensive Urban Education*. Boston: Pearson, 2006.

Lynch, Eleanor, and Marc Hanson. *Developing Cross-Cultural Competence: A Guide for Working with Young Children and Their Families*, 2nd ed. Baltimore: Paul Brooks, 1999.

Maniates, Helen, Betty Doerr, and Margaret Golden. *Teacher Our Children Well: Essential Strategies for the Urban Classroom*. Portsmouth: Heinemann, 2001.

Robles de Melendez, Wilma, and Verna Beck. *Teaching Young Children in Multicultural Classrooms: Issues, Concepts, and Strategies*. Albany: Delmar/Thomson Learning, 2007.

Sheets, Rosa Hernandez. *From Remedial to Gifted: Effects of Culturally Centered Pedagogy: Theory into Practice* 36, no. 3, 1995.

Sheets, Rosa Hernandez. *Diversity Pedagogy: Examining the Role of Culture in the Teaching Learning Process*. Boston: Pearson, 2005.

CHAPTER 5

HELPING STUDENTS

The fifth core value represented in the TEACHER acrostic is *Helping Students*. Help, as defined by Webster Dictionary, is to make it easier for someone to do something by offering one's services or resources. Some synonyms for help are ***assist***, *aid*, and *abet*. As the teacher reviews and analyzes the definition and synonyms for help, they must ask the following questions:

- What is meant by cultural sensitivity?
- Will each student be provided with scaffolding instructions?
- Does each student feel critical to the learning process?
- What motivation techniques will engage students in a classroom activity?

Demonstration of Cultural Sensitivity

Gordon and Browne[1] suggested "that cultural sensitivity means that each child's heritage is honored, unique from other cultures, and that it is respected." It means teachers must become familiar with the cultural norms of the children in their classroom and the teacher must build bridges for the children to be able to relate to the dominant culture. Teachers should know that an individual family does not represent the totality of the culture.

Attempting to meet the needs of these students who are unique and require diverse teaching and learning practices can be overwhelming. Sensitivity to their needs plays a major role. As an example, for students who are English Language Learners (ELL) or who come from an environment that is not considered enriched, it is essential that the teacher refers to the "All About Me" profile that was discussed in Chapter 2 to ensure that their students'

---

1. Ann Gordon and Kathryn Browne, *Beginnings and Beyond Foundations in Early Childhood Education*, 98.

needs are identified and properly addressed (Templates 2 and 3: All About Me).

As the teacher considers all the differences, it is highly recommended that scaffolded instructions be applied since this methodology would be greatly beneficial to various groups of students. Displaying pictures in English and other languages benefits ELL students and also helps other students by introducing them to a new language and teaching new words or reinforcing familiar ones.

There are also different socioeconomic groups in the classroom and, instead of feeling that one group is more knowledgeable than the other, the teacher may introduce and reinforce skills that could enhance all of the student groups. For some students, these skills may have already been taught at home and are being reinforced at school. Seeing a connection between home and school encourages parents and family members to have more conversations with their child about what happens at school instead of feeling that the school environment is a separate and foreign part of their child's experience[2]. For other students, many skills may be novel; however, the use of introduction and reinforcement enables the teacher to level out the educational learning field. This methodology leaves no child behind while building equity in the learning process. The idea of providing students with new information gives them confidence in learning. This methodology also demonstrates respect and appreciation for each student. Also, the teacher ensures that there will be equity in the learning process for all students in any classroom setting.

The students' racial and cultural backgrounds must also be acknowledged and considered in the teaching process. If a teacher happens to be in a classroom that does not have much cultural diversity, it is important to first teach the students about their own culture and then to follow that with lessons on other cultures. The idea is to give students a global experience so that they become familiar with and gain an appreciation for the diversity of cultures around them.

Klein and Chen[3] stated that "understanding an individual's culture is often the key to understanding the individual." Traditionally, the dominant motivation for Western preschool children was to maximize the differences

---

2. Karen Nemeth, *Many Languages, One Classroom: Teaching Dual and English Language Learners*, 17.
3. Diane Klein and Deborah Chen, *Working with Children Culturally Diverse Backgrounds*, 24.

between themselves and other children by outperforming them.[4] Cooperation and altruism are not highly valued in mainstream culture, whereas, for many non-mainstream groups, cooperation within the group and avoiding standing out among one's peers are more characteristic values. Some non-mainstream children either avoid outperforming their peers or help their peers to improve their own performance.

In the event the teacher does not know where to begin with regard to teaching diverse cultures, it is important for them to learn about "themself." This is the first step in being effective when teaching diversity. Moving forward, it is essential to both recognize and appreciate the diversity of cultures inside and outside the classroom. A four-pronged paradigm should be applied; the teacher must have a good understanding of their own culture, their own biases, their students' cultures, and the cultures that exist outside the classroom.

Even though teachers would not ordinarily be expected to know the characteristics of every culture, initial information can be obtained from parents, people, and organizations who are representative of the specific cultures in the classroom. Maps and globes can be used to show the geographic landscape. In addition, the specific cultural days that are scheduled by many schools, which include food demonstrations, artifacts, and clothing, can be highly beneficial to the school's community. However, it is important to continue to recognize the student's culture throughout the school year with varying activities that may include: the dissemination of cultural information; pictures that identify specific cultures; speakers from different cultural backgrounds; appropriate educational culture-specific movies or videos; and field trips to museums or other related outings. This four-pronged paradigm and cultural integration reflects the importance of, and appreciation and respect for, each student and their family (Template 14: The Teacher's Cultural Paradigm). This can be considered to be the beginning of the building block for equity in education.

Scaffolding Instructions

Feldman[5] stated that scaffolding is assistance or structuring provided by others. Scaffolding is the support provided for learning and problem solving

---

4. George Knight and Spencer Kagan, "Development of Prosocial and Competitive Behaviors in Anglo American and Mexican American Children", 1385-1394.
5. Robert Feldman, *Child Development: A Topical Approach*, 184.

that encourages independence and growth.[6,7,8,9] Scaffolding involves helping children think about and frame a task in an appropriate manner.[10] The early childhood theorist, Vygotsky[11] explained that "the process of scaffolding not only helps children solve specific problems but also aids in the development of their overall cognitive abilities." Lev Vygotsky's,[12] cited by Feldman,[13] Social Development Theory (Sociocultural Theory) includes one principle of scaffolding instructions. His theory maintains that providing a special type of help assists learners to move towards new concepts, skills, or understandings. This theory states that assistance to the learner is more beneficial than having the students find the answers to problems independently.

In teaching and learning, when a student is not able to find the appropriate answer, it can be frustrating. Students may not be able to move forward with assignments because they have been impeded with something they do not know. The idea of students' knowing that they can always seek assistance without being penalized or reprimanded makes a huge difference for their learning curve. Sometimes, students just need reassurance, simple clarification, or more in-depth information or training on a specific concept. As the teacher begins analyzing their techniques related to teaching and learning, they should realize the positive difference it makes to the classroom environment if students are always able to get clarity about any concepts without feeling belittled, fearful, or insecure when asking for more information.

Sometimes, when a teacher is explaining the concept of a math problem, it can appear to be extremely easy to the students. They may feel they

---

6. Sadhana Puntambekar and Roland Hubscher, "Tools for Scaffolding Students in a Complex Learning Environment: What Have We Gained and What Have We Missed", 112.
7. Panela Blewitt et al., "Shared Book Reading: When and How Questions Affect Young Children's World Learning", 101.
8. May Jadallah et al., "Influence of a Teacher's Scaffolding Moves During Child-Led Small-Group Discussions".
9. Stuart Hammond et al., "The effects of Parental Scaffolding on Preschoolers' Executive Function".
10. Robert Feldman, *Child Development: A Topical Approach*, 184.
11. Vygotsky 1997, cited by Robert Feldman, *Child Development: A Topical Approach*, 184.
12. Lev Vygotsky's 1978, cited by Robert Feldman, *Child Development: A Topical Approach*, 32-33.
13. Robert Feldman, *Child Development: A Topical Approach*, 32-33.

understand all the steps or the necessary sequences to provide the correct answer. However, once they sit down to complete the assignment, they can become confused, they might not know where to begin or, in some cases, they may not know how to reach the final steps. The idea of a student knowing that help or clarification for any form of uncertainty related to assignments is always available without any negative repercussions can be extremely comforting and rewarding. Of course, teachers are sometimes unable to address a student's issue because of the conflicts that are present when attempting to complete their teaching modules in a timely manner. There are two procedures the teacher should consider: obtaining volunteers to help students with concepts that are problematic, and re-teaching the concepts.

It is often necessary to give teachers assistance to meet the needs of their students. If teachers find they have insufficient help, they may want to consider soliciting volunteers from parents or the community to support their work. The volunteers may be able to administer spelling tests, read language assignments, or move around the classroom ensuring that the students are on task. While the volunteers are overseeing these tasks, the teacher could take the time to reteach concepts or a lesson with a group of students who have questions or found the assignment difficult. Sometimes, it is difficult for parents to assist in the daytime because of work schedules, but the teacher should still make inquires because some parents may have flexible working hours or ample leave that they can use. Community volunteers can be helpful because they may be retired teachers or school principals who are prepared to assist the school. Another useful idea is to work with the school's principal to earmark the money resulting from fund raising efforts for tutoring to build equity in the education program. Volunteerism is great, but a stipend would be an added incentive for outsiders to assist in the classroom.

Sometimes, teachers must be willing to reteach some lessons. If there are more than three students who do not understand specific concepts, the teacher must be willing to reteach the concepts using different methodologies and preferably hands-on techniques as a means of reinforcement. When there are less than three students who do not understand the material, the teacher may want to spend some time reteaching these specific students on an individual basis. This provides a perfect opportunity to use students who understand the material to explain it to the other students. Sometimes, peers may be more effective in conveying concepts to each other than adults.

The teacher must also be willing to accept that every lesson taught can always be improved sometimes by using different techniques or approaches. One prominent example is considering the Theory of Multiple Intelligences because it enables the teacher to implement activities designed to address students' different learning styles (Template 11). Also reviewing the students' "All About Me" profiles will remind the teacher of how the individual students learn, thereby enabling them to build on their students' strengths (Templates 2 and 3).

Each Student Feels That They are Critical to the Learning Process

The students must feel critical to the learning process because this allows them to reach their optimal potential. The teacher needs to ensure that the learning process is equitable and that students are at the center of learning in the classroom.[14] There is a variety of strategies to infuse a positive creative learning environment in an urban classroom. "Much of this creation is informed by the teacher's own background experience and his or her personality, but a key component, no matter what teacher differences exist, is that students must be given varied, contextualized, and meaningful opportunities to learn".[15]

It would be beneficial for the teacher to review the "All About Me" profile to help meet the needs of the students (Template 2 and 3). This is the first assignment that demonstrates to the students that they are important, and that learning is key to meeting the curriculum's objectives, goals, and outcomes. The teacher has recognized that each student is unique, and the teaching factors in the learning styles of each student are based on the information from their profiles.

Shade[16] reviewed a wide range of literature related to the cultural styles of African Americans, Asian Americans, American Indians, Latinos, and European Americans. She summarized four major suggestions to help teachers use both culture and cognitive styles in their teaching:

- Include multisensory presentations to open all pathways to the brain.

14. Andrea Stairs, Kelley Donnell, and Alyssa Dunn, *Urban Teaching in America: Theory, Research, and Practice in K-12 Classrooms*, 43.
15. Andrea Stairs, Kelley Donnell, and Alyssa Dunn, *Urban Teaching in America*, 43.
16. Barbara Shade, *Culture, Style, and the Educative Process*.

- Accept and understand different behavioral styles that could otherwise lead to unwarranted discipline problems.
- Restructure the classroom social environment to make it more inclusive and less exclusive.
- Include a variety of communication and thinking styles to strengthen information processing for all students.

In implementing the Theory of Multiple Intelligences, the teacher can provide academic assistance to each student who requires accommodations to move forward in the curriculum. Equity is provided throughout the learning process by recognizing how each student learns and by providing opportunities to meet all of their individual academic needs.

Maniates, Doerr, and Golden[17] maintained that a community of learners is created when the teacher knows their students as people as well as their individual interests, values, and daily experiences. Subsequently, students will do their best because the learning environment has shown they are the major focus at the center of how concepts are taught as all learning abilities have been considered (Template 11). Students will reach their maximum potential and not feel demeaned, undervalued, or mistreated. The self-fulfilling prophecy of prejudging students because of the color of their skin will have been eliminated from the classroom.

Although teachers may have to continue teaching concepts and moving forward with the curriculum, they will have developed a community of learners that will result in positive student outcomes. Additional volunteers, tutors, and peers can assist the teacher to ensure that all of students' learning styles and strengths/weaknesses are being accommodated. Instead of the classroom being centered on gifted students or those with the highest grades, the focus should be on each student to help each reach their maximum potential. This way, each student's uniqueness is being acknowledged, all students are viewed as important, and all efforts have been made to meet their diverse needs.

---

17. Helen Maniates, Betty Doerr and Margaret Golden, *Teacher Our Children Well: Essential Strategies for the Urban Classroom,* 34.

Motivation Techniques for the Teachers

Kopetz, Lease, and Warren-Kring[18] state some of the following beliefs that create continuous motivation in the classroom:

- All students can succeed in school.
- Students' interests are the highest priority in instruction; they are encouraged to share their own experiences.
- Praise, reinforcement, encouragement, and guidance reap rewarding student gains and benefits.
- Enthusiasm for and valuing students and their ideas boost the students' aspirations.
- Social connections and relationships are coveted.
- Care and concern are genuine, even when discipline is rendered.
- Teachers and students demonstrate a willingness to empathize with students' expressions of feelings.
- Students' ideas are heard and valued in the classroom.
- Students' or teachers' raised voices in the classroom are unbecoming and inappropriate.
- Classroom activities offer success to students, which encourages further effort.
- Opportunities are created that encourage all students to participate.
- Admirable student performance in classrooms is continually and consistently commended.
- The students' privacy is respected and can be shared with the teacher in confidence.
- Students are encouraged to be active and to identify with the school, thereby instilling a sense of belonging.
- School members attend community cultural events to learn more about the students.
- The students' strengths must be capitalized on to promote strong self-esteem.

Daily sincere compliments can demonstrate to children how important they are in the community of learners. Sometimes, the teacher may forget that students have the same feelings as adults. For an adult, a compliment is accepted for a new outfit, a new hairstyle, or losing a considerable amount

---

[18] Patricia Kopetz, Anthony Lease, and Bonnie Warren-Kring, *Comprehensive Urban Education*, 200-201.

of weight. If an adult goes to great lengths to make an improvement, they want to be acknowledged. This is the same for students.

Every day, the teacher must make sure to compliment students when appropriate and let them know that they have been noticed. The compliments must be sincere as an insincerity runs the risk of fragmenting any bond that is being developed between the teacher and student. The teacher must attempt to make every day positive, even if they may have to artificially create a positive scenario for some students to be given an acceptable compliment. A compliment can be verbal or physical such as a pat on the back after an excellent response to a question. A kind gesture is also appropriate.

Unacceptable behavior must also be acknowledged when necessary so that students are aware of what will be tolerated in the classroom. When a student responds to a question and their answer is wrong, the teacher may immediately say, "No, that is not the correct answer." The student could find this response very embarrassing and demeaning. Teachers should consider responding to an incorrect answer with a different question to show a relationship and to draw out the correct response. The teacher can also use the following type of responses: "not quite," "can anyone else help with the question," or "what is another way of explaining the answer." The teacher must consider that, once a student has felt embarrassed in class, they may find it difficult to participate in other class discussions. When students are treated fairly without being humiliated, they will accept that it is okay to try, even if the answer is incorrect. They will feel empowered to continue thinking and participating fully in class. Sometimes, even though the answers may not be correct, the cognition that is involved is thought provoking. Wrong answers can demonstrate that the students are thoroughly involved and that they want to learn and share the knowledge they have acquired. There is a strong correlation between cognition and intellectual development.

The idea of students thinking outside the box can be reflective of the knowledge that they have acquired. It is important that the teacher ensures students know the importance of classroom engagement, even though their answers may not always be correct. The answers could indicate what the students are thinking, and the most important thing is putting the students on the right track.

This approach is also analytic and allows the student to be involved with classroom sharing and the integration of knowledge. When students feel comfortable, happy, and confident, they will continue to thrive educationally. An environment in which students do not always have to be right and feel comfortable trying and taking risks is important. This approach is not only building confidence, it is also demonstrating equity in education and allowing students to reach their maximum potential.

Students will model their teacher's behavior. The teacher, therefore, needs to be positive, nurturing, and enthusiastic which will create the same atmosphere in the classroom environment. Students absorb the energy that their teachers display in the classroom. The classroom environment created by the teacher will positively encourage and support each student in the classroom; it will also assist the students in portraying the same, or similar, behavior as the teacher with their classmates. The idea of including group activities demonstrates to students that their environment is supportive, and their peers are friends who should be respected and appreciated. When students are being unkind to one another, either physically or verbally, teachers should be proactive and inform them that the classroom is to be a happy, kind, and safe place for all students. Additionally, teachers must provide students with socialization lessons and activities on treating others as they would want to be treated. Of course, the classroom rules may be referred to while reinforcing appropriate behavior. These rules are immensely helpful in keeping order in the classroom.

Once the teacher has demonstrated equity in the classroom and the rules are posted for all to see, the students should be encouraged to refer to them when necessary. The teacher must assure the students that the classroom environment will be adaptable and secure for each child. Further, when students are not getting along, these rules will sometimes help them to resolve issues among themselves. However, if one of the students tells another that they are not following a specific rule and if they do not handle certain situations immediately and appropriately, then the teacher should intervene. Instructing students to apologize is appropriate, but the apology must be sincere. It is appropriate for the students involved in the issue or misbehavior to discuss what happened and to come up with an appropriate resolution. If the students are too young to resolve the issue, the teacher must intervene and assist in resolving the issue.

A student's interactions with their classmates should be supportive and respectful. When students are working on group projects, each student should have their own role to play while also being encouraged to help each other, if needed. Often, peer intervention can be more influential than the teacher's, and it is a helpful tool that enables the teacher to ensure that all students are improving and attempting to understand the learning concepts presented. Some students will be able to understand these learning concepts better in a group situation, which supports the saying that "two heads are better than one." The teacher should organize strategies that support students and ensure that the only time a student needs to work alone is when the teacher is assessing an individual's skill levels.

Chapter Summary

The teacher can ensure that students will meet their maximal potential by demonstrating sensitivity to each one. The teacher should use a four-pronged paradigm that includes learning about the teacher's own culture and biases, the student's culture, and cultures outside the classroom. This paradigm is the foundation for building equity in the classroom (Template 14).

In teaching and learning, students knowing that they can always ask for help with assignments, without being penalized or belittled, could make a huge difference in their learning curve. Giving teachers the necessary assistance to scaffold instructions is critical. The assistance can be in the form of volunteers, tutors, parents, or other community members.

Building on students' strengths, implementing the Theory of Multiple Intelligences, and using the "All About Me" profile can provide tools for academic assistance for each student (Templates 2, 3, and 12). Daily, sincere verbal compliments help to create a positive learning environment. Making all answers acceptable, even when they may not be "right," enables the students to think outside the box. The implementation and application of these suggestions will demonstrate that students are the major focus of the learning environment.

References

Blewitt, Pamela et al. "Shared Book Reading: When and How Questions Affect Young Children's World Learning". *Journal of Educational Psychology*, 101, no. 2 (2009): 294-304.

Feldman, Robert. *Child Development: A Topical Approach*. Upper Saddle River: Pearson, 2014.

Gordon, Ann, and Kathryn Browne. *Beginnings and Beyond Foundations in Early Childhood Education*, 8th ed. Boston: Cengage Learning, 2011.

Hammond, Stuart, et al. "The effects of Parental Scaffolding on Preschoolers' Executive Function". *Developmental Psychology*, 48 (2012): 271-281.

Jadallah, May et al. "Influence of a Teacher's Scaffolding Moves During Child-Led Small-Group Discussions". *American Educational Research Journal* 48, no. 1 (2011): 194-230.

Klein, Diane, and Deborah Chen. *Working with Children Culturally Diverse Backgrounds*. Albany: Delmar/Thomson Learning, 2001.

Knight, George, and Spencer Kagan. "Development of Prosocial and Competitive Behaviors in Anglo American and Mexican American Children". *Journal of Cross-Cultural Psychology*, 48 (1977): 1385-1394.

Kopetz, Patricia, Anthony Lease, and Bonnie Warren-Kring. *Comprehensive Urban Education*. Boston: Pearson, 2006.

Maniates, Helen, Betty Doerr, and Margaret Golden. *Teacher Our Children Well: Essential Strategies for the Urban Classroom*. Portsmouth: Heinemann, 2001.

Nakamura, Raymond M. *Healthy Classroom Management: Motivation, Communication, and Discipline*. Belmont: Wadsworth/Thomson Learning, 2000.

Nemeth, Karen. *Many Languages, One Classroom: Teaching Dual and English Language Learners*. Beltsville: Gryphon House, 2009.

Ormrod, Jeanne Ellis. *Educational Psychology, Developing Learners*, 4th ed. Upper Saddle River: Pearson, 2003.

Puntambekar, Sadhana, and Roland Hubscher. "Tools for Scaffolding Students in a Complex Learning Environment: What Have We Gained and What Have We Missed?" *Educational Psychologist* 40, no. 1 (2005): 1-12.

Shade, Barbara. *Culture, Style, and the Educative Process*. Springfield: Charles C. Thomas, 1989.

Stairs, Andrea., Kelley Donnell, and Alyssa Dunn. *Urban Teaching in America-Theory, Research, and Practice in K-12 Classrooms*. Thousand Oaks: Sage, 2012.

Vygotsky, Levi. *Mind in Society: The Development of Higher Psychological Processes*. Cambridge: Harvard University Press, 1978.

Vygotsky, Levi. *Educational Psychology*. Delray Beach: St. Lucie Press, 1997 (Original work published 1926).

CHAPTER 6

EQUALIZING OPPORTUNITIES
FOR EVERY CHILD

The sixth core value represented in the TEACHER acrostic is *Equalizing Opportunities* for every child. The Webster Dictionary defines "equalizing" as making the same in quantity, size, or degree throughout a place or group; equalizing also includes the quality of being fair and impartial. Synonyms for equalizing include equal, equate, justice, and even-handedness. Other terms for equalizing are making the same and implying fairness. The teacher should answer the following questions when equalizing opportunities or providing equity to ensure that fairness is entrenched throughout the classroom:

- How can authentic assessment be an asset to equalizing students' academic achievements?
- How can teachers equalize opportunities for each child?
- What can teachers implement to ensure that dual language learners (DLL) and immigrant students are being treated equitably?
- How can building on a student's strengths be fundamental to building equity in the classroom?

Authentic Assessment and Students' Academic Achievements

Standardized tests in schools have demonstrated that children of color generally lag behind their White counterparts. It is inequitable to have one major indicator, such as test scores, to decide how students are excelling in their academic subjects. Children have diverse interests and strengths in different subjects; therefore, the teacher is obligated to analyze the "All About Me" profile for each student to determine their strengths and weaknesses along with their individual learning styles (Templates 2, 3, and 11).

When students' interests and strengths have been identified, they can be used to establish and institute learning that is unique for each child within the general curriculum. Cooper[1] affirmed that authentic performance assessment techniques get closer to how students apply knowledge rather than being concerned with how knowledge is stored in their minds.

Educators and the business community have placed emphasis on schools to teach higher order thinking skills, such as critical thinking and problem-solving. As a result, some educators have called for a different type of assessment that directly measures actual student performance. For example, if teachers want to know how well a student writes, then they can review writing samples. If a teacher wants to know how well students understand scientific concepts, then the students can complete a science experiment. These assessments measure how well students understand a concept or skill by what they are able to demonstrate rather than relying on them to choose the correct response on a multiple-choice test.

Cooper[2] stated that portfolios are one method of authentic assessment which can be used to measure the students' work. Teachers can have separate portfolios for math, reading, and science. The ideal is to have work samples at the beginning, middle, and the end of each semester. This collection of portfolios will demonstrate the growth the students exhibited throughout the semester or year.

Howe and Lisi[3] suggested that schools and classroom teachers examine their assessment systems to ensure equity for all learners. With authentic assessments, the focus is on the application of skills and knowledge instead of just knowledge. Howe and Lisi[4] suggested using multiple authentic assessments for students. Einbender and Wood[5] reported that authentic assessments involve the application of skills to a task that requires students to go beyond the instructional context and connect meaningful problems with the outside world. In contrast, standardized tests have more artificial tasks that are deliberately created rather than natural or spontaneous ones.

---

1. Ryan Cooper, *Those Who Can, Teach*, 396.
2. Ryan Cooper, *Those Who Can, Teach,* 396-397.
3. William Howe and Penelope Lisi, *Becoming a Multicultural Educator: Developing Awareness, Gaining Skills and Taking Action*, 304.
4. William Howe and Penelope Lisi, *Becoming a Multicultural Educator,* 304.
5. Lynne Einbender and Diane Wood. *An Authentic Journey: Teachers' Emergent Understandings About Authentic Assessment and Practice*, cited in William Howe and Penelope Lisi, *Becoming a Multicultural Educator,* 295.

Howe and Lisi[6] noted that, although there are different formats for authentic assessments, there are three characteristics that are common:

- Daily observations through student engagement and the progress of their learning.
- Involvement of students in the self-assessment.
- Grounding of students in the content and learning standards rather than standardization.

The researchers Howe and Lisi[7] provided a checklist for the development of culturally responsive assessments, which includes the following 14 points:

1. Reflect student experiences. Develop assessments that reflect student experiences in and outside of the classroom.
2. Attend to students' learning styles. Construct assessment tasks that accommodate and relate to the students' learning styles and their ways of thinking.
3. Convey expectations clearly to students. Make sure that the students understand what they have to do, and consider the language and terms used in case examples are needed or terms need to be defined.
4. Provide ample time for students to complete the assessment.
5. Provide multiple ways for students to demonstrate their learning. Always use more than one assessment to evaluate the students' learning.
6. Provide clear performance standards. Let the students know before the assessment that they are being assessed on knowledge, skills, the development of a product, or reasoning. Provide an example of what "excellence" looks like.
7. Tap into higher order thinking skills. Provide multilayered problems that must be solved by applying knowledge and skills. Emphasize what the learners know and can do.
8. Balance formative and summative assessments. Educators should provide formative assessments that are not high stakes and clear, immediate, and useful feedback to the students regarding their progress.
9. Connect evaluation to instruction. Use the results of assessments to enhance instructional design to improve performance for every learner.

---

6. William Howe and Penelope Lisi, *Becoming a Multicultural Educator*, 295.
7. William Howe and Penelope Lisi, *Becoming a Multicultural Educator*, 294.

10. Provide choice in assessments. When possible, give the students to an opportunity to demonstrate what they have learned.
11. Develop assessments collaboratively in teacher teams. Work with colleagues in ongoing professional development to ensure proficiency in interpreting and scoring alternative assessments.
12. Provide for the disaggregation of data. Teachers should disaggregate data into specific groups that may be of interest or concern. The assessment report will show gaps as well as specific areas in which diverse students perform well.
13. Report instructional strategies that appear to work. Assessment data should not report on student performance but on instructional strategies that are and are not working instead.
14. Share the results with interested people. Share assessment data with parents, students, and the community every week.

Implementing these 14 points when developing assessments for students is critical to ensuring that they are meeting the needs of all their students. If students do not understand a word or need clarity on any question, this checklist may help to support them. Using various authentic assessments and correlating them with how students learn can contribute to making a positive difference in the accuracy of skill and knowledge. Therefore, if students are unfamiliar with a teaching term and they, as a result, get the whole question wrong, then there has not been an accurate evaluation of their knowledge.

Authentic assessments may be in the form of oral presentations, written essays, portfolios, or other creative measures. These assessments go beyond formats such as matching, true and false, or filling in the appropriate word. Authentic assessments allow students to be assessed according to their individual learning styles. If the teacher knows each student's learning style and their interests, the assessments can be developed according to the students' comfort level and how they present and affirm information. If the student has been provided with some degree of scaffolding, a follow-up assessment may be given as part of an authentic assessment to demonstrate that the student has learned the information, can apply the skills, and can retain the required knowledge. If the student has not performed satisfactorily, then more support needs to be given.

Equalizing Opportunities for Every Student

Stairs, Donnell, and Dunn[8] define learning opportunities to mean:

- that individual teachers, whether required by national, state, or local standards, must provide opportunities for every student to learn in their classrooms;
- guaranteeing that all students have access to the same high-level courses and materials so they can achieve the same high standards and access good career opportunities;
- that the teachers are provided with adequate time to teach content and real-life skills;
- that they use this time wisely to ensure that their students are able to engage in mastery learning; and
- that the teachers encourage and model diversity, respect, and collaboration.[9]

Resources are needed to ensure that all students are provided with equal opportunities such as offering additional tutoring after school, asking parents or community helpers to assist students who may need some additional support, or requiring the student teacher or teaching assistant to help students in need of additional reinforcement. Any additional help for students should be introduced and shared as extra learning tools in the curriculum. In this way, additional help is not viewed as embarrassing or demeaning to students. The additional help could be labeled as reinforcing specific concepts. When the same concept is introduced using multiple strategies, a different technique can often help the student understand it. The teacher should have a group of volunteers made up of parents, members of the Parent Techer Association, grandparents, or community participants who may be retired teachers. Schools should have a policy for volunteers that requires an application that includes, but is not limited to, a fingerprint background check and medical clearance, such as tuberculosis test results. Of course, safety is always the first concern; teaching students and teachers must ensure that the appropriate volunteer protocol is followed.

---

8. Andrea Stairs, Kelley Donnell, and Alyssa Dunn, *Urban Teaching in America: Theory, Research, and Practice in K-12 Classrooms,* 31-32.
9. Wendy Schwartz, 1995, *Opportunity to Learn Standards: Their Impact on Urban Students*, cited by Andrea Stairs, Kelley Donnell, and Alyssa Dunn, *Urban Teaching in America*, 106.

Derman-Sparks and Edwards[10] maintain that the following suggestions will impact children's experience of acceptance in the classroom and result in successful learning:

- Have the same high expectations for children from every family.
- Pay attention to each child's unique learning style. Instead of looking for what children do or do not know, adapt activities to support their strengths.
- Create beautiful environments for all children.
- Be mindful of concerns about clothing. Make or buy aprons. Buy cheap men's shirts that can be worn during art or other messy activities. Do a clothes swap so parents can exchange clothes that their child has outgrown.
- Be cautious about activities that help the poor but can unintentionally convey messages of superiority.
- Use sensory materials that are not food. For many families, food is a precious resource. Bird seed may be used instead of rice or cornmeal.

Teachers can develop and implement parent workshops where parents come to the classroom and help make personalized booklets, costumes for classroom skits, picture cards, math flashcards, or games in order to provide diverse activities which engage students with hands-on activities. These skill-directed active engagement workshops for parents help equalize opportunities in and outside the classroom by giving parents tools they can use at home when resources are limited.

Klein and Chen[11] addressed two points that explain why equal opportunity and access do not mean that everyone is alike. The first point is the importance of valuing diversity which, for young children, means pointing out that differences are interesting and positive. Mainstream America tends to be uncomfortable with differences. Somehow there is confusion with equal opportunity and sameness. The teacher must find ways to demonstrate sameness and differences. Differences should be noted as important and interesting, and they should be incorporated into the curriculum. The second point is for early childhood professionals to acknowledge their own biases and discomforts when dealing with children's ethnic and racial identities and biases. There is a tendency to ignore these issues but, when teachers

---

10. Louise Derman-Sparks and Julie Olsen Edwards, *Anti-Bias Education for Young Children and Ourselves*.
11. Diane Klein and Deborah Chen, *Working with Children Culturally Diverse Backgrounds*, 126-127.

take the opportunity to prevent normal concerns and attitudes from becoming ingrained prejudices, these biases and discomforts may become open to change. Children's concerns and attitudes are intense, and it therefore becomes important and necessary for their teachers to demonstrate an appreciation and respect for differences.

Treating Dual Language Learners (DLL) and Immigrant Children Equitably

Imagine being in a classroom where no one looks like you, no one speaks your language, no one understands you, and, as a result, no one acknowledges you. Often, students who are immigrants and dual language learners (DLL) find themselves in this kind of situation. Additionally, their parents may be unable to communicate effectively with teachers on their children's behalf because of the language barrier. This is when the teacher really needs to demonstrate that the individual classroom is an equitable environment.

Boutte[12] declares that, since each child is unique, multicultural teachers must discover specifics about children and their families that facilitate learning and development. She recommends the following components for multicultural classes:

- Modeling by the teacher: The teacher should model acceptance of others. Children will emulate this attitude and therefore value people who are different. The teacher should not allow children to tease others about their culture or language.
- Multicultural heritage: The curriculum should include music, art, science, and other things that represent different cultures.
- Multicultural literature: The teacher should use literature and textbooks that represent children with different racial characteristics, ethnic backgrounds, home circumstances, and physical and mental differences.[13]
- Multilinguistic experiences: Children should learn different words that represent the same thing. For example, asking children how many ways they know how to greet someone in a different language.

---

12. Gloria Boutte, *Multicultural Education: Raising Consciousness*, 60-77.
13. Laura Smolkin and Joseph Sunia, *Exploring a "Multicultural" Award-Winning Book: Multiple Traditions, Multiple Perspectives, Multiple Pedagogies*, cited in Gloria Boutte, *Multicultural Education: Raising Consciousness*, 64.

- Involvement of people from different cultures: The teacher should involve people with different characteristics and backgrounds in classroom activities, such as parents, representatives of various cultural groups, and members of the community (e.g., local merchants).[14]

If teachers are unfamiliar with their students' cultures, then they need to learn about the customs and practices. The teacher can make sure that DLL, immigrant and other children of color are acknowledged, respected, and appreciated daily. The teacher can accomplish this task by making sure these students continue to participate in classroom activities. To facilitate this, the teacher may have to assign students appropriate jobs that allow for student participation. When parents/families are invited to school, the teacher should extend a special invitation to parents of DLL and immigrant students. When students have a difficult time understanding certain concepts, the teacher should make sure that scaffolding is used to provide additional assistance so that all students can stay on task and feel included in all activities. Sometimes providing partners for the students can also help to make them feel that they are a part of the classroom activities. When parents who do not speak English arrive at school for a meeting or parent/teacher conference, it is beneficial to have an appropriate interpreter present.

Having parents/family come into the classroom and share their culture provides excellent learning experiences. A warm welcome must be given to these parents, who may also bring artifacts to share, and teachers should be allowed to serve some light refreshments on these occasions. The idea of sharing some prior knowledge about the parents' culture can also be greatly beneficial for the students. This knowledge prepares the students for the visit while demonstrating their importance. The teacher may also encourage students to ask the visiting parents questions. After parents visit the class, the teacher is encouraged to conduct follow-up lessons using two activities. First, have the students write thank you notes to the parents for sharing their culture and letting them know what they have learned from their visit; and second, require the students to make art projects, including writing or video compositions, related to the cultural presentation to highlight the impactful nature of the visit. These activities demonstrate the teacher's efforts to understand their students' cultures and they make students feel that they are

---

14. Margaret Lay-Dopyera and John Dopyera, *Becoming a Teacher of Young Children*, cited in Gloria Boutte, *Multicultural Education: Raising Consciousness*, 60.

valued, appreciated, and respected. Likewise, the parents will feel a part of each student's classroom and they also will feel valued and respected. The students in the classroom are indirectly learning that each student and their cultural differences are valued, which will automatically set an equitable tone in the classroom.

Teachers can invite parents of all of the students in the class to share their cultures. This could be a monthly activity. The teacher may need to invite a few parents at a time to come to the classroom until all of the parents have been accommodated. Thereafter, the teacher will develop a schedule starting with immigrants and DLL students. Of course, this cultural parental activity at the beginning of the school year is a way of offering support to students in their new classroom environment so that they feel included and welcomed.

Building on the Students' Strengths is Fundamental to Building Equity

Some students may come to school with harrowing experiences, which may include exposure to poverty, crime in their neighborhoods, a lack of proper nutrition, responsibility for their younger sibling's preparations for school, as well as having to perform other adult tasks. These circumstances make it difficult for them to concentrate and stay on task when learning. Of course, these circumstances cannot be controlled by the teacher, but teachers can be instrumental in helping their students with the various school tasks. Although it is the students' responsibility to accomplish their individual tasks, if the teacher discovers that there are obstacles beyond a student's control that prevent the completion of these tasks, the teacher will need to provide further assistance to help the student to move forward, in spite of these obstacles. When teachers realize that some students do not have support at home to assist with homework, they should develop a designated time for students to complete their homework and provide students assistance for them to understand the concepts and correctly complete the assigned tasks.

Cochran-Smith[15] maintained that focusing on the following six principles forms the important work of socially just teaching practices:

1. Support meaningful academic work within communities of learners when implementing social justice.

---

15. Marilyn Cochran-Smith, "Learning to Teach for Social Justice".

2. Build on what students bring to school with them: knowledge and interests, cultural and linguistic resources.
3. Teach skills and bridge gaps.
4. Work with, and not against, individuals, families, and communities.
5. Diversify modes of assessment.
6. Make activism, power, and inequity explicit parts of the curriculum.

In addition to the teacher practicing Cochran-Smith's six principles, it is necessary that they refer to the Student's Profile that was completed at the beginning of the school year to develop and build on their students' strengths. The teacher must remember that the circumstances that students experience in their lives can deter them from moving forward academically. Teachers are critical to helping students move forward, even in the presence of other hurdles they face. The students' resiliency when making the effort to excel can be accomplished with the support of teachers who are aware of the existing barriers and are able to help the students navigate through these obstacles to acquire knowledge, skills, and the determination to move forward academically.

Students recognize teachers who are nurturing, sincerely interested in their well-being, and continuously demonstrating empathy for them. These teachers will usually be rewarded by their students' positive efforts to excel. Their teachers' care and encouragement will become the students' backbone and strength in their academic pursuits.

Chapter Summary

Teachers should use authentic assessments to demonstrate the growth in academic performance that students have experienced throughout the semester. Using a variety of assessments, both oral and written, will focus on diverse learners' skills and knowledge.

Teachers should ensure that high quality opportunities are provided for every student and they must give every student access to high-level courses, materials, and content aligned with developmentally appropriate skills. There must be adequate time to execute teaching and to engage every child so that they can master the learning concepts.

Parents are an integral part of the process and should be involved in skills directed workshops to engage students. Teachers and other educators must recognize their own biases to prevent them from becoming ingrained prejudices that hinder change in attitudes toward their students. Teachers must provide diverse resources and opportunities in an equitable classroom environment for DLL, immigrants, and other students. Although some students have encountered difficult circumstances, teachers must provide the necessary support for them while building on their strengths so they can be academically successful.

References

Boutte, Gloria. *Multicultural Education: Raising Consciousness*. Belmont: Wadsworth Publishing, 1999.
Cochran-Smith, Marilyn. "Learning to Teach for Social Justice". In *The Education of Teachers: Ninety-Eighth Yearbook of the National Society for the Study of Education*, edited by Gary Griffin, 114-144. Chicago: University of Chicago Press, 1999.
Cooper, Ryan. *Those Who Can, Teach*. Boston: Wadsworth, 2010.
Derman-Sparks, Louise, and Julie Olsen Edwards. *Anti-Bias Education for Young Children and Ourselves*. Washington: NAEYC, 2012.
Einbender, Lynne, and Diane Wood. An Authentic Journey: Teachers' Emergent Understandings About Authentic Assessment and Practice. New York: Columbia University Teachers College, 1995. (ERIC Document Reproduction Service No. ED384585).
Howe, William, and Penelope Lisi. *Becoming a Multicultural Educator: Developing Awareness, Gaining Skills and Taking Action*. Oakland: Sage, 2020.
Klein, Diane, and Deborah Chen. *Working with Children Culturally Diverse Backgrounds*. Albany: Delmar/Thomson Learning, 2001, 126-127.
Lay-Dopyera, Margaret, and John Dopyera. *Becoming a Teacher of Young Children*, 3rd ed. New York: Random House, 1987.
Schwartz, Wendy. *Opportunity to Learn Standards: Their Impact on Urban Students*. New York: ERIC Clearinghouse Digest Number 110 on Urban Education, 1995. https://files.eric.ed.gov/fulltext/ED389816.pdf.
Smolkin, Laura, and Joseph Sunia. (1999). *Exploring a "Multicultural" Award-Winning Book: Multiple Traditions, Multiple Perspectives, Multiple Pedagogies*. The New Advocate: 1999.
Stairs, Andrea., Kelley Donnell, and Alyssa Dunn. *Urban Teaching in America-Theory, Research, and Practice in K-12 Classrooms*. Thousand Oaks: Sage, 2012.

CHAPTER 7

REFLECTING ON EQUITABLE PRACTICES

The seventh core value in the teacher acrostic is *Reflecting on Equitable Practices*. Reflecting is necessary for the teacher to know what has worked with each child and which lessons and opportunities need to be revised to meet everyone's needs. Reflection enables the daily activities to be reviewed in order to make improvements on segments of the lesson that may need to be altered. Reflection will only be effective if it is practiced throughout the day. Several questions should be asked as the teacher reviews and reflects on the daily activities in the curriculum including:

- Did the daily activities meet the needs of every student in the classroom and build on the students' strengths?
- Are there indicators to demonstrate that the classroom activities are equitable?
- Is the teacher using families/parents, the community, and administrators to enable every student to reach their optimal potential?
- How is the teacher developing and implementing a reflective journal?

Daily Activities that Build on Students' Strengths

At the end of each day, the teacher must review the lessons taught. Stairs, Donnell, and Dunn[1] stated that reflection and inquiry are cyclical processes whereby one question or wondering triggers many more questions. The teacher must determine ways to put their thoughts into an action plan. Often teachers and others in education believe that reflection is a natural process, but reflection must be learned and practiced over time. York-Barr, Sommers, Ghere, and Montie[2] revealed that reflective practice involves teachers taking

---

[1] Andrea Stairs, Kelley Donnell, and Alyssa Dunn, *Urban Teaching in America-Theory, Research, and Practice in K-12 Classrooms*, 115-116.
2. Jennifer York-Barr et al., *Reflective Practice to Improve Schools: An Action Guide for Educators*, cited in Andrea Stairs, Kelley Donnell, and Alyssa Dunn, *Urban Teaching in America*, 116-117.

a deliberate pause from their everyday activities; maintaining an open perspective; engaging in complex thinking processes; examining their beliefs, goals, and practices; developing new insights and understandings; and taking actions that improve students' learning. In support of these points, Howe and Lisi[3] suggest that effective teachers reflect individually and in collaboration with colleagues about what they teach, why they teach in particular ways, and how they can improve their teaching. This type of reflection means teachers are setting aside time regularly to consider their strengths and weaknesses and setting both short-and long-term goals for self-improvement.

When the teacher observes that some students are not on track with the concepts being taught, the teacher needs to review the students' profiles, begin to determine what the students' interests are, and ask how the lesson can be taught differently so that these students can learn the concepts more effectively. The teacher may realize that a hands-on activity will help some students, while another group may need to be taught something, such as a rhyme, that will assist them in remembering the steps to accomplish the task. A different group of students may benefit from being taught with manipulatives, whereby they can use movement or their sense of touch to accomplish their goals. It must be remembered that young students learn through their senses, and the use of these different modalities and strategies to implement the various learning styles in the classroom enables each child to learn the concepts.

An example of a teacher teaching one lesson while incorporating Multiple Intelligences Theory with different learning styles (Templates 11 and 12) benefits teaching numbers. The concept of teaching numbers 1–10 enables the students to count, recognize numbers, and match them to the appropriate items. It is important to remember that the teacher should introduce one concept at a time to young children. The assumption in this lesson is that the students have been assessed and that most can count and recognize numbers. The next step is to introduce matching the numbers to the appropriate number of items. The following resources are examples of ways to incorporate Multiple Intelligences into this lesson:

- Cards with the number on one side and the corresponding number of objects on the back of the card. (Note: for the visual learner, objects

---

3. William Howe and Penelope Lisi, *Becoming a Multicultural Educator: Developing Awareness, Gaining Skills and Taking Action*, 326-237.

should be easily identified so the student can label their names, which allows language development to be incorporated with math).
- The student can make their own cards with numbers and objects. (Note: for the kinesthetic learner, the student could be given 10 individual cards to create their own numbers and objects. They could trace, draw, color, or cut-out and paste pictures or small objects on the cards. In addition, the students could use sand to glue on the numbers).
- Singing familiar tunes like the Alphabet Song. The students can sing the numbers shown on the card and/or count the objects on the reverse side of the card. (This applies to students who are musical intelligence learners).

Of course, all these activities have a verbal-linguistic component because, upon completion of the activity, the student would have to say the number, match the number to the objects, and label the objects. Depending on the age of the students, they could provide a descriptive sentence related to the objects.

Reagan et al.[4] stated that the teacher cannot rely solely on instinct alone or on prepackaged sets of techniques to justify the selection of instructional strategies. Rather, the teacher must engage in reflection about their own practice and realize that good teaching requires reflective, rational, and conscious decision making.

Indicators of Equitable Classroom Activities

Howe and Lisi[5] (2020, 337) indicated that teachers make many decisions based on a particular set of beliefs, values, expectations, experiences, and life histories. These beliefs may ignore, contradict, or conflict with the students' beliefs, values, and life histories. As a result, reflective practice becomes essential. It counteracts the tendency to call on the same students to respond to questions, to volunteer for tasks, to be the leader for various activities in the classroom, and to be afforded special opportunities.

Teachers should make a list of all the students in their classroom and identify the tasks in which they participated. In this way, the teacher can

---

4. Timothy Reagan et al., *Becoming a Reflective Educator: How to Build a Culture of Inquiry in the Schools*, 2nd ed., cited in William Howe and Penelope Lisi, *Becoming a Multicultural Educator*, 333.
5. William Howe and Penelope Lisi, *Becoming a Multicultural Educator*, 337.

rotate tasks, classroom duties, and opportunities. This rotation should be arranged by the teacher on a weekly basis with a written schedule highlighting the names of students and their specific tasks corresponding to the weekly dates. This will ensure that every student has the same opportunities. The schedule will be used by the teacher to be inclusive of every student in the classroom. This equity demonstrates to the students that they are valued and respected. It also sets the tone for each student to acknowledge that their teacher is modeling equity, which is inclusive of all students. Students will notice this modeling and they will begin to emulate this behavior toward their classmates. Previously, some students may have never participated in the classroom in this capacity. Students who have behavior problems or who may not be at the top of the class academically will now be recognized in a positive manner. As the teacher reflects on each student's behavior or classroom performance, the student's response to the assigned task will provide the teacher with feedback on the student's strengths. Finally, an equitable playing field will be provided for every student in the classroom.

Teachers should ensure that their classrooms are equitable by demonstrating that classroom activities incorporate their students' cultures. Robles de Melendez and Beck[6] suggested that " the child is the most important source for planning multicultural activities, and the multicultural classroom curriculum should be child-centered and designed to effectively respond to the needs of both culturally diverse and mainstream children." The researchers noted that a welcoming environment tells children and their families that their cultures and ethnicities are valued and respected.

The emergence of multicultural education in the United States began with a belief in equality by providing opportunities to all individuals regardless of their social background. Public education in the United States has been built on this premise; however, in many instances over the last two decades, opportunities have been denied to children in many of our communities. Children have not been equally served and appropriately equipped classrooms and resources have been lacking even after the 1954 mandate in Brown vs the Board of Education. This mandated granted full access to equal school opportunities and affirmed that segregated schools do not provide equal opportunities. Today, the justification behind the reform movement underpins multicultural education. Through reflection, teachers can determine if they are equitably addressing every student's the needs,

---

6. Wilma Robles de Melendez and Verna Beck, *Teaching Young Children in Multicultural Classrooms: Issues, Concepts, and Strategies*, 304.

diverse learning styles, and backgrounds as they implement differentiated strategies.

Using Families/Parents, the Community, and Administrators to Enable Every Student to Reach their Maximum Potential

Teachers must remind parents that they are the students' first teachers. Students really benefit from a collaborative effort between their parents and the teacher. This effort forms a seamless bond between home and school, making students aware that their parents will be duly notified about whatever happens at school. The teacher might even schedule conferences with students and their parents to ensure that all stakeholders are on the same page working to make sure students can reach their optimal potential.

The community can be a vital resource for both the teacher and the students. Westheimer and Kahne[7] noted that professional development opportunities should expand teachers' roles as members of caring communities by incorporating cultural-immersion activities. Such activities include visiting students' homes, exploring their communities, interviewing residents and community leaders, and researching the history of their students' communities.

Community-related field trips can be incorporated into the disciplines of the school curriculum. Students could then be exposed to diverse areas of the community, a variety of services, a multitude of professions, and cultures and ethnic groups from around the world. Targeted field trip sites might include businesses such as a college, a dentist or a doctor's office, a grocery store, a drug store/pharmacy, a veterinary office, a restaurant, a bank, an art/music studio, and a supply warehouse. The personnel in these places of businesses could share their stories of inspiration and success with the students, provide information about their occupations, and give tours of their facilities. Follow-up lessons should address several areas of the curriculum. Language activities could include identifying and discussing the vocabulary introduced during the field trip or retelling or writing about what the students learned (language experience chart). Math, science, or social studies activities can involve counting, such as the number of new things the student experienced, or discussing the importance and purpose of each business. Arts-related activities could involve making-up songs or drawing pictures showing students' experience and capturing their feelings

---

7. Joel Westheimer and Joseph Kahne, "Building school communities: An experience-based model".

about the trip. Physical education activities could involve acting out a story related to an experience on the trip or developing a guessing game where one student portrays different actions related to the trip. The idea of infusing the students' communities into the curriculum bridges home and school and incorporates the realistic, everyday experiences of life into learning for the students. These types of learning opportunities demonstrate that students' environments are relevant to their academic experiences which reinforces the idea that learning becomes more interesting and engaging to students when they are exposed to hands-on experiences (Template 15: Field Trip).

Derman-Sparks, LeeKeenan, & Nimmo[8] identified "an ally is a person or group who shares and strives to implement your anti-bias values, supports and publicly endorses your anti-bias efforts, understands the challenges involved in the work, and provides access to resources and networks." Often, these allies become the true collaborators and take on leadership tasks. It becomes important for teachers to recognize their allies in the community and the school, as well as among colleagues and families. Derman-Sparks, LeeKeenan & Nimmo[9] cited an example of a Latino community center as an excellent ally in the community which could provide teachers with access to Spanish translation services and information on local cultural celebrations.

Teachers can build a partnership with parents and other staff to help every child develop freely and fully. Gordon & Browne[10] explained that this partnership will be fully operational and functional when teachers partake in the following measures:

- Help parents to feel welcome at school and to become a part of the learning process.
- Give parents information on childrearing and provide emotional support.
- Show parents they are respected for their unique contribution to their child's learning.
- Make sure that their contact with parents is not only limited to problem situations, but that it is also inclusive of positive feedback.

---

8. Louise Derman-Sparks, Debbie Lee Keenan, and John Nimmo. *Leading Anti-Bias Early Childhood Program: A Guide for Change*, 45.
9. Louise Derman-Sparks, Debbie Lee Keenan, and John Nimmo, *Leading Anti-Bias Early Childhood Program*, 48.
10. Ann Gordon and Kathryn Browne, *Guiding Young Children in a Diverse Society*, 227.

- Take the time to understand the parents' cultural, social, ethnic, and religious backgrounds.
- Provide multilingual communications, as needed.
- Listen to parents' concerns.
- Involve parents in meaningful ways in the classroom and in advisory and policy-setting committees.
- Be sensitive to individual family structures and needs.

These measures are important as they enable teachers and parents to embrace the students' needs and will provide the best support for children to achieve their optimal potential.

Administrators are teachers' critical allies that help them move forward with meeting the needs of each child. However, Kopetz, Lease, and Warren-Kring[11] suggested that school principals must believe in the shared decision making that is a part of the overall school culture. Unfortunately, many teachers believe that shared governance is lacking in their schools. School reform is impossible in this kind of environment.

In Chapter 1, "Time for Change," four high schools were highlighted because of their significant gains in bridging the achievement gap They demonstrated that one of the key components was the strong support of their school administrators. Principals had high expectations of staff, as well as students, and administrators helped to achieve these expectations through professional development and flexible schedules that provided longer blocks of time to facilitate instruction in critical content areas. In these schools, the teachers and administrators discussed the importance of aligning the curriculum with the state and district standards and tests. Two members of staff from the schools used the alignment process along with an examination of test scores and classroom observations when deciding which standards were most critically in need of being addressed. In addition, the staff from all the schools examined the performance of a subpopulation of students to determine which reading and math topics needed to be reviewed and taught differently.

Douglas[12] maintained that leadership conduits should demand a new way of thinking for greater access to high-quality leadership development programs and formal leadership pathways and pipelines. Douglas indicated field-wide

---

11. Patricia Kopetz, Anthony Lease, and Bonnie Warren-Kring, *Comprehensive Urban Education*, 150.
12. Anne Douglas, *Leading for Change in Early Care and Education*, 65.

leadership development ecosystem that cultivates leadership for change and innovation from within the early care and education fields is also needed. Taking a path that has not been taken before, trying a new idea, or thinking about problems in new and radical ways requires creativity and courage. Kelley and Kelley[13] wrote that "Creativity is something you practice, not just a talent you're born with."

Teachers should take time to reflect on how they can effectively use families, community, peers, and administrators. This enhances the creative process which benefits the educational development of each child.

The Teacher Develops the Reflective Journal

Cooper[14] suggested that the most important aspect of school encounters are guidance and experiences that provide data for reflection. Students will get the most out of the learning experiences when teachers have reflected on what they have taught in a manner that ensures this happens.

Reflection is the process of reviewing what has been taught and the demonstrated results and then identifying the additional actions needed to engage every student. Webster Dictionary defines reflection as serious thought or consideration. Teachers reflect during and at the end of the day. It is important to write these reflections down because they provide thoughts, self-assessments, and critiques that improve the teacher's effectiveness in the classroom. Sometimes the lessons that are taught may not be engaging for some students as they may be too easy or too challenging. Reflection helps a teacher to know what should be taught next or the modifications that are needed. After the teacher presents and reflects on a lesson, some questions may emerge, such as the following:

- Were the students engaged?
- Does the lesson need to be taught in a different way for some students?
- What can be done in the lesson to support students who are having difficulty learning the concepts?

---

13. Tom Kelley and David Kelley, "Reclaim Your Creative Confidence", *Harvard Business Review*, cited in Anne Douglas, *Leading for Change in Early Care and Education*, 65.
14. Ryan Cooper, *Those Who Can, Teach*, 12.

- How many different strategies should be provided to meet the needs of all the students who require support or differentiated instruction?

Taking the time to think about and brainstorm responses to these questions promotes awareness of what is effective, what is ineffective, and how to make changes to yield positive outcomes.

Taggart and Wilson[15] explained that reflective thinking or practice can be accomplished through a variety of activities, such as action research, case studies, and observations. However, Howe and Lisi[16] noted that the most widely used form of reflection is journaling. Kouzes and Posner[17] supported the development of a dialogue journal in which one writes about events and activities and receives regular written feedback from, or participates in, a discussion with a mentor or interested colleague. Kouzes and Posner[18] explained that the dialogue journal should include details about an event (date, who was involved, and an explanation of what happened) in order to analyze it within its context and an explanation of what the writer learned.

Cooper[19] described reflection as the most important method of professional development. All teachers, both new and old, must systematically reflect on what is happening in their classroom on a regular basis. Cooper cites the following questions that teachers must ask during and at the end of the day:

- What went right in class today?
- What did not work?
- Which students am I not teaching, and what should I do about it?
- What can I do to get make my uninvolved students more engaged?
- Are there other ways of presenting this material that will connect with students who have different learning styles?

15. Germaine Taggart and Alfred Wilson, *Promoting Reflective Thinking in Teachers: 44 Action Strategies,* cited in William Howe and Penelope Lisi, *Becoming a Multicultural Educator*, 334.
16. William Howe and Penelope Lisi, *Becoming a Multicultural Educator*, 330.
17. Jim Kouzes and Barry Posner, *The Leadership Challenge,* cited in William Howe and Penelope Lisi, *Becoming a Multicultural Educator*, 334.
18. Jim Kouzes and Barry Posner, *The Leadership Challenge,* cited in William Howe and Penelope Lisi, *Becoming a Multicultural Educator*, 334.
19. Ryan Cooper, *Those Who Can, Teach,* 518.

He concludes by emphasizing that teachers who are reflective practitioners are headed toward excellence in teaching as they have developed the habit of systematic reflection on their work.

Chapter Summary

Reflection is the process of reviewing what has been taught, the demonstrated results, and identifying the additional actions needed to engage every student. Reflection must be practiced daily to be an effective tool for education. When collaborating, teachers can use the time to reflect with colleagues, thereby improving their teaching skills. Reflection is a technique that helps teachers analyze their strengths and weaknesses so that they can identify and achieve short- and long-term goals for self-improvement. Reflection is not natural; it must be learned and intentional.

Teachers need to reflect on questions, actions, and the resulting outcomes as they perform their duties and review their own performance in providing an equitable learning environment for every student. Teachers must review the students' profiles and incorporate their learning styles to demonstrate support for each student. Teachers must be intentional about student engagement with all activities. The teacher should have a schedule listing the classroom duties and which students have been selected for specific opportunities to ensure that opportunities are spread evenly among everyone.

Teachers should be intentional about involving administrators and initiating parent/family and community partnerships. The partnerships should be fully operational and functional. Administrators are needed for their expertise in leadership and to be supportive of changes that may be needed to develop an equitable environment for every child.

The reflective journal can be the most important tool for professional development, and it can help students to reach their maximum potential. This journal allows the teacher to meet the academic needs of every student by analyzing what the students have learned, what worked well when teaching the lessons, and what improvements are needed for each student to achieve their optimal potential on a daily basis.

References

Cooper, Ryan. *Those Who can, teach*. Boston: Wadsworth, 2010.

Derman-Sparks, Louise, Debbie Lee Keenan, and John Nimmo. *Leading Anti-Bias Early Childhood Program: A Guide for Change*. New York: Teachers College Press and Washington: NAEYC, 2015.

Douglas, Anne. *Leading for Change in Early Care and Education*. New York: Teacher's College Press, 2017.

Gordon, Ann, and Kathryn Browne. *Guiding Young Children in a Diverse Society*. Needham Heights: Allyn & Bacon, 1996.

Howe, William, and Penelope Lisi. *Becoming a Multicultural Educator: Developing Awareness, Gaining Skills and Taking Action*. Oakland: Sage, 2020.

Irvine, Jacqueline Jordan, et al. (2006). *Comprehensive Urban Education*. Boston: Pearson Education, 2006.

Kelley, Tom, and David Kelley. "Reclaim Your Creative Confidence". *Harvard Business Review* (December 2012). hbr.org/2012/12/reclaim-your-creative-confidence.

Kopetz, Patricia, Anthony Lease, and Bonnie Warren-Kring. *Comprehensive Urban Education*. Boston: Pearson, 2006.

Kouzes, Jim, and Barry Posner. *The Leadership Challenge*, 4th ed. San Francisco: Jossey-Bass, 200

Reagan, Timothy, Charles Case, and John Brubacher. *Becoming a Reflective Educator: How to Build a Culture of Inquiry in the Schools*, 2nd ed. Thousand Oaks: Corwin Press, 2000.

Robles de Melendez, Wilma, and Verna Beck. *Teaching Young Children in Multicultural Classrooms: Issues, Concepts, and Strategies*. Albany: Delmar/Thomson Learning, 2007.

Stairs, Andrea, Kelly Donnell, and Alyssa Dunn. Urban Teaching in America-Theory, Research, and Practice in K-12 Classrooms. Thousand Oaks: Sage, 2012.

Taggart, Germaine, and Alfred Wilson. *Promoting Reflective Thinking in Teachers: 44 Action Strategies*. Thousand Oaks: Corwin, 1998.

Westheimer, Joel, and Joseph Kahne. "Building school communities: An experience-based model". *Phi Delta Kappan*, 75, no. 4 (1993), 324-328.

York-Barr, Jennifer et al. *Reflective Practice to Improve Schools: An Action Guide for Educators*. Thousand Oaks: Corwin, 2001.

CHAPTER 8

SUMMARY

Time is the first core value that will help to bridge the achievement gap for children of color so they can fully compete in the modern workplace. This has led to key educational developmental concepts being discussed by researchers in the United States. The 2005 U.S. Department of Education Report[1] has shown the way forward regarding the achievement gap using research data collected from four high schools across the country that have intentionally begun to close the achievement gap. Some common themes for improvements reported were high expectations for students, eliminating remedial classes, recommending minority students enroll in honor courses in advance, and providing learning support for students, such as tutoring and study skills programs that provide personalized attention on an on-going basis.

Research has demonstrated that the teacher is the most important component in bridging the achievement gap. It is essential for teachers to recognize and to be honest about their own biases. It is also important to know what their biases are, so they can move forward and acquire the core values to build equity in the classroom and close the achievement gap.

**Engaging Students** is the second core value. The "All About Me" profile is a questionnaire regarding the students' characteristics that should be sent home for parents to complete. This information is valuable for teachers. It gives teachers a developmental account from the parents' point of view, as they are the child's first teachers. The purpose of the profile is for the teacher to get to know their students. Teachers can also use it to personalize the curriculum by incorporating some of the children's beliefs and values into it.

The teachers can also send home a profile that describes themselves so that the parents can get to know who is teaching their children. This profile creates a mini biographical sketch that will help parents, families, and the

---

1. Cameron Brenchley, "Equity and Excellence Commission Delivers Report to Secretary Duncan".

student to bond with their teacher, and it also provides a critical way for teachers to appreciate and respect the students' differences, values, and beliefs.

Parents/family involvement is necessary to help close the achievement gap, and early childhood education professionals must provide information and strategies to non-mainstream parents to enable them to have various ways of interacting with their children that help close the literacy gap, as literacy is the cornerstone of the curriculum. When parents know that the teacher is sincerely interested in their children's academic achievement, this interest creates a special bond between the parents and their children. When a classroom environment has been built on family expectations, it helps the teacher to build and develop positive self-esteem in their students. As a result, the classroom becomes an extension of the home.

When concepts from the "All About Me" profile are implemented into the classroom's foundation, it will demonstrate how important every child is and how their cultural background will underpin what and how they learn in the classroom.

Students may not do well on standardized tests because of a lack of testing skills, a lack of nutrition, environmental issues, and test anxiety. To offset this, teachers can use both authentic and non-traditional assessments. Keeping healthy snacks and drinking water in the classroom can help to manage the students' physical needs.

Appreciating Students is the third core value. Through the students' profiles, the teacher can discern their strengths and what makes them happy. Therefore, observations and reflections are important criteria on the developmental continuum for the full comprehension of the strength and happiness criteria. This is important for teachers to provide the necessary supportive learning environment for developing students.

The idea of being valued and appreciated should filter through all classroom activities, as well as to the students' social development. Teachers must ensure that they complement students on a daily basis in order to model positive behaviors for the students to create and support their self-concept, which is essential in teaching and learning. Once students have a positive self-concept, it will give them confidence in the learning environment and help them to overcome any obstacles that they may encounter. Teachers can present activities that demonstrate value, inclusion, and equity. When students know that they are critical to the whole learning process, they feel a part of the learning environment.

Communicating is the fourth core value. The teacher's goal should be to build a well-rounded student, who is fully developed socially, emotionally, physically, cognitively, and intellectually. These domains are critical in reaching the students' optimal potential and the teacher can refer to the students' profiles as data that helps the teacher develop a classroom environment that will be both interesting for the students and meet their individual needs.

The goal of personalizing the curriculum to make learning fun can occur if teachers incorporate their students' interests as part of teaching and learning. Rather than focusing on what students do not know or what they do not like, teaching should be geared to the children's strengths and, therefore, focus on building on challenging concepts that reflect the students' interests and likes. To support the students, therefore, three learning styles can be applied. These styles are visual learning, auditory learning, and tactile learning.

Each individual student's data from the profile sheets should be reviewed and used to incorporate their interests into the curriculum as well as to integrate their multiple intelligences; reviewing and implementing student's data will minimize challenges that the students may face. When students have bonded with their teacher, the learning environment becomes an ideal situation for both the teachers and the students. The students should know that they will be in a happy, safe, and cared for place while they are being taught.

Teachers should also provide students with oral compliments and encouragement about the accomplishments or improvements they have made during the day. Challenges that occur during the day can be collectively addressed by the students and it is important that they come up with solutions to address issues. At the close of the day, the students should share their reflections or solutions with the class. They will learn that reflection can become a way to solve situations as well as to prepare themselves to endure the next challenge.

Teachers should be mindful that parents are the students' first mentors; therefore, teachers and parents should be encouraged to mix through inclusive classroom activities. Teachers should make sure the classroom is a place where parents are welcomed and, if there is a language barrier, the school can arrange for interpreters to be present at all activities. When teachers accommodate parents and include them in classroom activities, a sense of trust between them is created and demonstrates respect for the parents/family.

The teacher's attitudes are critical components in the education process as they are inculcated in their demonstration of a positive attitude towards every child in the classroom. The teacher should demonstrate that both student and their cultures are important, so it is necessary for teachers to learn about all of these different cultures in order to accommodate all students. The positive attitude of the teacher really gives students a feeling of belonging and of wanting to meet the learning objectives established in the classroom curriculum.

__Helping Students__ is the fifth core value. Teachers will notice that the classroom will lend itself to diverse learning styles and, because of this, it is recommended that scaffolded instructions be applied as a teaching methodology that is especially beneficial for teaching English Language Learners (ELL) and children of color.

Teachers must also acknowledge the linguistic, racial, and cultural differences in the classroom. The teacher can begin with teaching about the students' different cultures and then expand to other cultures. This type of teaching experience demonstrates an appreciation and respect for cultural differences; it also provides students with new global information that gives them confidence.

Students need to know that they can always receive the necessary assistance to understand the concepts that have been taught without feeling any negative repercussions from their teacher. The teacher, in turn, will need to collaborate with parents/families, principals, and the community to provide tutoring and volunteering resources. Teachers should recognize that different strategies may be used to teach the same lesson and the Theory of Multiple Intelligences can be one such strategy that can be used in the curriculum, since it addresses the students' diverse learning styles. Again, compliments from their teacher can encourage students to excel and provide evidence of the teacher's genuine interest in their well-being. The teacher should remind their students of the importance of classroom engagement and that, even when an answer is incorrect, their cognitive development is being strengthened.

Equalizing Opportunities for every child is the sixth core value. Teachers should go beyond standardized testing and implement authentic assessments. Children of color often do not do well on standardize testing, whereas authentic assessments provide a variety of measures that can assess concepts even though students have diverse learning styles. Diverse assessments demonstrate growth in the student's academic performance.

Teachers must ensure that all students have access to high-level courses, materials, and resources. Adequate time must be provided in the schedule to execute teaching and to engage every child so they can master the learning concepts. Parents/families can be a critical resource by making hands-on materials available that can be used to teach various concepts to build an equitable classroom. Teachers must recognize and resolve their own biases. Teachers must provide diverse resources and opportunities for diverse language learners (DLL), immigrants, and every child of color to ensure an equitable classroom environment. Teachers must build on students' strengths so that they can move forward academically.

Reflection is the seventh core value in the acrostic. Teachers should reflect during and at the end of the day. Teachers can record notes during the day so that they will be available at the end of the day. Reflection is critical so that the teacher can implement diverse strategies specific to students' different learning styles. Teachers must engage in reflection about their own practice in order to realize that reflective teaching requires reflective, conscious decision making.

Students really benefit from a collaborative effort between their parents/families and their teacher. This effort makes the education process seamless and ensures that all stakeholders, including fellow colleagues, are on the same page and working to ensure that all students reach their maximum potential. Teachers should attempt to relate students' prior experiences to learning, since this will make learning concepts more familiar and interesting.

A reflective journal can be the most important tool for professional development as it allows teachers to analyze what they have learned on a daily basis, what works well in the teaching lessons, and what improvements must be implemented for each student to excel.

APPENDIX

CHAPTER TEMPLATES

Template 1 through 15 can be used by the teacher for the lessons that have been discussed throughout the chapters. The teacher can tweak the specific templates to accommodate the age and diverse learning styles of the students in the classroom.

Template 1: The Blueprint for Education

The Seven Core Values 　1.　Time for Change 　2.　Engaging Students 　3.　Appreciating the Students' Cultures 　4.　Challenging Students 　5.　Helping Students 　6.　Equalizing Opportunities for Students 　7.　Reflecting on Equitable Practices in the Classroom
Collaboration 　•　Parents/Caregiver 　•　Family 　•　Community
Respecting and Appreciating Diverse Learning Styles 　•　Visual Learner 　•　Auditory Learner 　•　Kinesthetic Learner
Empowering Students and Teachers 　•　Engaging Students 　•　Implementing Differentiated Strategies 　•　Recognizing, Appreciating, and Respecting every Student's Cultural Background 　•　Interweaving the Core Values with the School, the Student, and the Family

Template 2: All About Me

Name of Child:
Birthdate of Child:

1. What is your favorite color?
2. What do you like to do for fun?
3. Do you have a pet?
4. Do you have brothers and sisters? If so, what are their names and ages?
5. What is your favorite food?
6. What do you like best about school?
7. What is your favorite subject in school?
8. If you could meet anyone in the world, who would it be?
9. What kind of music do you listen to?
10. When you grow up, what do you want to be?

Template 3: All About Me

Hello, my name is _____.
I was born on _____.
I live in _____.
My favorite food is _____.
I like to _____,
and my favorite hobbies are _____,

_____, and _____.
I laugh and smile when _____.
I get angry or sad when _____.
I like to go to a lot of places, but my favorite is
_____.
When I grow up, I want to be _____.

Template 4: Child's Picture Book

All About Me

I live in Washington, DC

My favorite food is tacos

My favorite subject in school is math

Template 5: Meet the Teacher

Hi! My name is Ms. Monroe and I am going to be your second-grade science teacher. This will be my second-year teaching science and I am looking forward to all the new discoveries and experiments for the school year.

I am from Washington, DC and lived here my whole life. I have two siblings, an older brother and younger sister. I love spending time with my family. I do not have any children now and that is fine because I can spend some time traveling. I have been to the Bahamas, Aruba, and some places in the United States, but would like to travel more.

I cannot wait to spend the next year learning and growing with you!

My Favorites

Food: Pasta
Movie: Avengers
Book: Dr. Seuss Green Eggs and Ham
Color: Red
Drink: Iced Tea
Season: Winter
Animal: Wolf
Hobby: Cooking

Template 6: Daily Quick Health Check

Teachers should check each child as they enter the classroom. This daily check includes the following:

- Activity level, general mood, and behavior
- Discharge from nose, eyes, or ears
- Breathing difficulties, severe sneezing, or coughing
- Sores, rashes, or unusual spots
- Skin color (pale or flushed), swelling, or bruising
- This should be done by the teacher listening, looking, feeling, and smelling if there is something that is not the norm for that child.

If any of the above indicators are observed, the teacher should contact the parent and discuss their observations with them immediately. If the indicators are listed in the school or childcare exclusion policy, the parent should be notified to pick up their child and take the child home. If the observation does not dictate exclusion, the teacher and parent should discuss how the child should be managed for the day and at what point the teacher should notify the parent.

Source: Robertson, Cathie. *Safety, Nutrition, & Health in Early Education.* Boston: Cengage Learning, 2016.

Template 7 Observational Tools

OVERVIEW OF OBSERVATIONAL TOOLS

Methods for Collecting Observational Data

1. Narratives
    a. Anecdotal records
    b. Running records
    c. Learning center logs
2. Sampling
    a. Time sampling
    b. Event sampling
3. Rating Scales
    a. Graphic scales
    b. Rubrics
4. Checklists
    a. Developmental

Criteria for Observing Children

1.	**Objectivity**:	Be non-judgmental about each child.
2.	**Confidentiality**:	Information should not be shared.
3.	**Recording details**:	Record every detail.
4.	**Use direct quotes**:	Record exactly what the child says.
5.	**Using mood cues**:	Describe the child's emotional mood.

Template 8: Anecdotal Record

Anecdotal records are a popular method that is easy to use. They can be brief and used by the observer to describe an incident.

CHILD'S NAME: AGE: DATE:

OBSERVER: PLACE: TIME:

INCIDENT:

COMMENT:

Template 9: Teaching Fractions Using Pizza

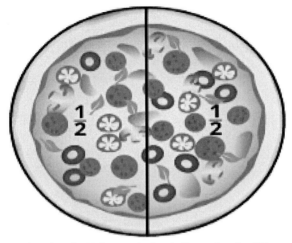

This Photo by Unknown Author is licensed under *CC BY*

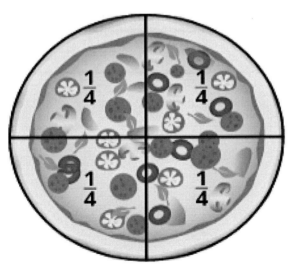

This Photo by Unknown Author is licensed under *CC BY*

Template 10: Favorite Ice Cream Flavor

What is your Favorite Flavor of Ice Cream?

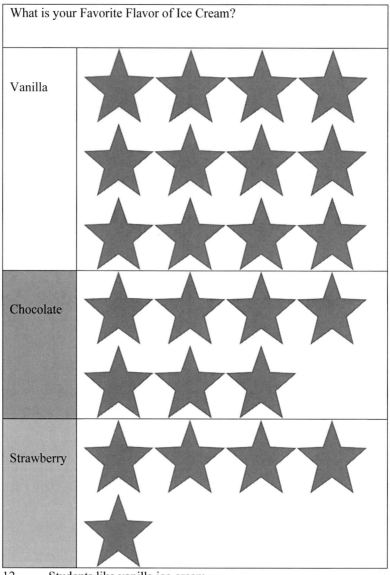

Vanilla	
Chocolate	
Strawberry	

12   Students like vanilla ice cream
7   Students like chocolate ice cream
5   Students like strawberry ice cream   Total Students: 24

Template 11: Learning Styles

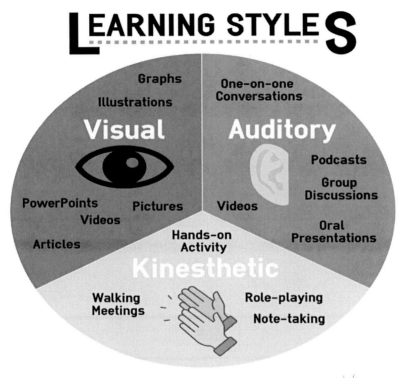

Hopehealth.com

Template 12: Multiple Intelligences

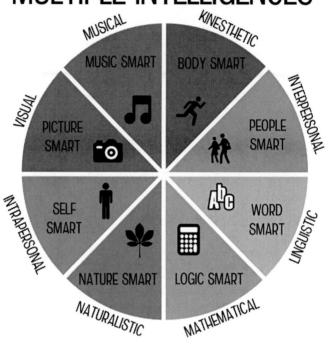

Template 13 Job Chart

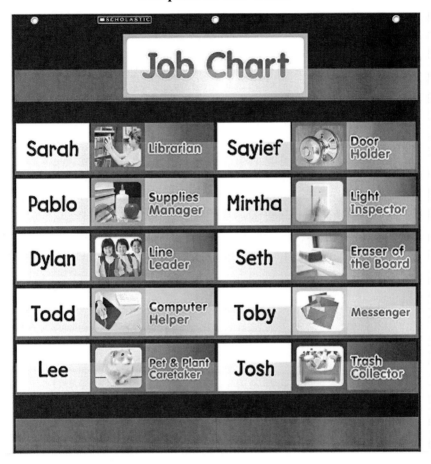

Template 14: Teacher's Cultural Paradigm

Template 15: Field Trip

My Field Trip

Name_____

Date _____

We went to: _____

I learned about:_____

_____

_____

_____

Here is a picture of something I saw:

Here is a picture of what I liked best:

INDEX